Y0-BSQ-430

THE FIVE POINTS
of CALVINISM

by

HERMAN HANKO
HOMER C. HOEKSEMA
GISE J. VAN BAREN

Reformed Free Publishing Association
P. O. Box 2006
Grand Rapids, Michigan 49501

The Five Points of Calvinism by Herman Hanko, Homer
Hoeksema, and Gise J. Van Baren, Copyright © 1976 by
Reformed Free Publishing Association. All rights reserved. No
part of this book may be used or reprinted in any form without
permission from the publisher, except in the case of a brief
quotation used in connection with a critical article or review. For
information address: Reformed Free Publishing Association,
Box 2006, Grand Rapids, Michigan 49501.

Library of Congress Catalog Card Number 76-471-66
ISBN 0-916206-14-9

Reprinted, 1980, 1988

Printed in the United States of America

30.42
194f

L. I. F. E. Bible College
LIBRARY
1100 COVINA BLVD
SAN DIMAS, CA 91773

CONTENTS

039363

FOREWORD

The five cardinal doctrines expounded in the chapters of this book are known to many as the Five Points of Calvinism, and to others as the "doctrines of grace." While these doctrines, though certainly not originated by John Calvin, were re-emphasized and taught anew by him at the time of the Reformation, it remained for the Synod of Dordrecht, 1618-19, which was convened to settle the Arminian controversy in the Reformed Churches of the Netherlands, to formulate these truths with great clarity and in painstaking detail. This official formulation was accomplished in a creed which represented the consensus of all Reformed churches of that day, the Canons of Dordrecht.

To this day, these doctrinal declarations have remained unaltered; and they continue to be a mighty bulwark against the heresy of Arminian free-willism, the danger of which is as great and greater than it was in the days of Jacobus Arminius himself.

The format of these chapters is accounted for by the fact that they were originally five popular lectures, delivered in 1966-67 in Grand Rapids, Michigan under the sponsorship of the Protestant Reformed Churches of that area.

The three authors are ministers in the Protestant Reformed Churches in America. Herman C. Hanko is professor of New Testament and Church History at the Theological School of the Protestant Reformed Churches; he has written Chapters 1 and 2. Homer C. Hoeksema is professor of Dogmatics and Old Testament at the same Theological School, and is the author of Chapter 3. Gise J. Van Baren is pastor of First Protestant Reformed Church of Grand Rapids, Michigan; and he is the author of Chapters 4 and 5.

May the Lord our God use these chapters for the instruction and enlightenment of many.

Chapter I

Total Depravity

Total Depravity

Herman Hanko

The doctrine of Total Depravity, with which this chapter has to do, is one of the "Five Points of Calvinism." It is not out of place, therefore, briefly to discuss the history of these five points.

Historically, the occasion for them is to be found in the Arminian controversy of the 16th and 17th centuries. At that time a certain man by the name of Jacob Arminius began to teach, in the Reformed Churches of the Netherlands, doctrines contrary to the Reformed faith and to Scripture. In the early part of the 17th century, 1610 to be exact, his followers, known then as the party of the Remonstrants, drew up five statements of doctrine in which they set forth their own views. They submitted these statements for the consideration of the Reformed Churches in the Netherlands in the hope that these statements would be adopted and approved.

It was not until the Autumn of 1618 that a General Synod of the Reformed Churches was called to consider these statements of the Arminians. At this Synod were present, not only delegates from the Reformed Churches in the Netherlands, but delegates from all the Reformed Churches on the continent of Europe. After careful consideration, these five points of doctrine presented by the Arminians were found to be contrary to Scripture and were rejected. But as an answer to these statements, our fathers, at the Great Synod of Dordrecht, set forth five doctrines which they considered to be the Scriptural and Confessional answer to the position of the Arminians. These doctrines have been put into the five Canons of Dordt and have become known as the five points of Calvinism.

The very fact, however, that these doctrines were called the five points of Calvinism proves that our fathers at Dordrecht did not consider these doctrines to be original with them. They were not, at that Synod, making any claims to developing doctrine. They consistently maintained the position that the Arminians had set forth doctrines which were contrary to the historic faith. And they, in answer to these Arminians, simply reiterated what had been the position of the Reformed Churches since the time of the Calvin Reformation.

In fact, our fathers at Dordrecht knew well that these truths set forth in the Canons could not only be traced back to the Calvin Reformation; they could be traced back to the theology of Saint Augustine who lived almost a millennium before Calvin did his work in Geneva. For it was Augustine who had originally defined these truths. Calvin himself, again and again, pays tribute to the work of Augustine and points out that what he is saying has been said before him by the Bishop of Hippo. The Synod of Dordrecht was conscious of this.

This is worthy of note because we ought to understand that the truth of total depravity, with which this speech has to do, is not a novel doctrine. It has a long and illustrious history. It has been the confession of the church since the Fifth Century after Christ. The fathers at Dordrecht, after they had formulated these truths, made a note of this in the conclusion of the Canons where this statement appears:

> This doctrine the Synod judges to be drawn from the Word of God, and to be agreeable to the Confessions of the Reformed Churches.

Now all this means that the truth of total depravity which has been confessed for a long time in the church of Jesus Christ has been part of the confession of the church because the church has always believed that this truth is founded upon the Word of God. This bears special emphasis. So often it happens that those who have serious qualifications about the truth of total depravity make these qualifications, not on the basis of the Word of God, but on the basis of personal observation. They look about them at their fellow men and they notice in their observations that they find apparently a great deal of good which men succeed in accomplishing apart from the power of sovereign grace. And on the basis of these observations, they come to certain conclusions which, in effect, deny the truth of total depravity.

But this is incorrect. It must be emphasized that this truth must not be formulated on the basis of our own personal observations. Rather this truth must be set forth as Scripture itself sets it forth. In other words, we must bow before the sovereign, infallible authority of Scripture. We must listen to God's sentence which He pronounces upon men and upon us. We must listen to what God has to say concerning our depravity. And only when we listen to what God has to say, shall we discover the truth concerning mankind in general and ourselves in particular.

There are three subjects which we must notice in our consideration of Total Depravity:

I. What Is Depravity?
II. What Is Meant by *Total* Depravity?
III. What Is The Importance Of This Doctrine?

I. What Is Depravity?

Before we enter into a discussion of the meaning of depravity as it is set forth in Scripture, it is important to survey briefly the history of this doctrine from the time of Augustine to the time of the Synod of Dordt. This history perhaps holds for us some surprises.

The occasion for Augustine's formulation of the truth of total depravity was the teaching of a certain Pelagius who appeared in Rome in the early part of the Fifth Century. He began to teach views which were totally at variance with Scripture. He taught that every child which is born into the world is born good, without any sin. In fact he insisted that every child was as good as Adam when he came forth from the hands of his Creator and before he ate of the forbidden tree. If you would ask Pelagius: "What is the explanation then for the fact that there is sin in the world?" he would answer: "That is to be determined by the choice which man is able to make either for good or for bad." His nature, Pelagius said, is inclined to the good. In fact there have been in the history of the world men who have lived their entire lives without sinning at all. But some people sin. And they sin because of the fact that they pick up from their fellow men bad habits. Sin therefore, in the view of Pelagius, is a habit. And as is true of any habit, the more a particular sin is committed, the stronger also the habit becomes. The more a man is guilty of one particular type of sin, the more deeply this habit becomes rooted in his nature. Nevertheless, sin always remains nothing more than a habit. And inasmuch as sin is only a habit, the solution to the problem of sin lies in the breaking of the habit. Nothing else. There is no need, Pelagius insisted, for salvation. There is no need for grace; much less for sovereign grace. All that a man has to do if he wants to break the habit of sin is have a firm enough resolve. By a choice of his own will he will presently succeed.

Augustine raised a long and loud protest against these anti-Scriptural views. Augustine himself knew better. And he knew better, on the one hand, because he had in his own life experienced something quite different. In his early life Augustine was very evil, even immoral. He had committed many grievous sins. He had learned from his own personal experience that sin was more than a mere habit. It was a vicious, destructive, and powerful force in man's very nature. And he had learned too, by the grace and mercy of God which he never ceased to extol, that the only possibility of deliverance from sin was through the power of sovereign grace.

And so, on the other hand, he found these truths set forth in Scripture. He insisted that while indeed Adam was created by God in a state of perfect righteousness, nevertheless the fall brought such consequences upon Adam and upon his posterity that man became totally incapable of doing any good at all -- of any kind. Augustine was so insistent on this point that he included in his condemnation the apparent good deeds of heathen men -- of heathen philosophers such as Socrates, Plato,and Cicero. He claimed that these deeds were not good in any sense of the word; that they were a perversion and corruption of the good; that the only power of doing good was to be found in the power of sovereign grace.

Now the views of Augustine did not prevail in the church of his time, except among a few. But there arose instead in the church a view which became known as Semi-pelagianism. The men who held these views did not want to go to the ridiculous and absurd extremes of Pelagius himself. And yet, at the same time, they did not want the system of Augustine either. They attempted a compromise. And as is true of all compromises, they only invented a new heresy. They taught that it is indeed true that a man who is born into the world is not good. He does not stand in the state in which Adam stood in Paradise before the fall. But while they insisted on that, they nevertheless also insisted on the fact that man was not totally depraved. They said he was sick. And indeed, while the kind of sickness which he had was a fatal sickness, so that if this sickness was not cured, presently it would result in death, nevertheless, in this period of sickness man was capable of accomplishing a great deal of good. Particularly, he was capable, by an exercise of his own will, to summon to his aid the Great Physican to come with the balm of healing grace to save him from his fatal disease. God on His part, said the Semi-pelagians, has prepared salvation for all men. He has prepared the cure for this malady which afflicts mankind. And God is also prepared to give this healing balm to all men. In fact, God even goes one step farther than this, and offers this balm to all men to be accepted or rejected by them. But beyond that, the Semi-pelagians insisted, God will not go. That healing balm will ultimately be applied to man to cure his

12

malady if man himself wants it. The whole matter of his cure therefore, of his salvation, turns upon the choice of his own will.

If this position of the Semi-pelagians sounds somewhat familiar to you and appears to you to be characteristic of much of modern day preaching, be assured of the fact that it is indeed an ancient heresy.

This whole system of Semi-pelagianism became the foundation for the doctrine of Roman Catholic work-righteousness. The whole imposing structure of Romish work-righteousness was founded foursquare upon this modification of Pelagianism.

It was not until the time of the Protestant Reformation that the truths which Augustine set forth were once more truths publicly proclaimed in the Church. Martin Luther began this. In opposition to Roman Catholic work-righteousness he saw that the whole structure of Semi-pelagianism had to be torn away and that the firm foundation of total depravity had to be set forth once more. And he insisted that so complete is that total depravity that even the will of man itself is completely enslaved by sin. He wrote a book about it. It is available today. It is called "The Bondage of the Will."

But it was John Calvin who set this truth forth in connection with all the truth of the Word of God and formulated this truth as it was expressed at the time of the Synod of Dordrecht. It is not necessary to go into detail regarding the teaching of Calvin. Anyone who is at all acquainted with Calvin's writings (especially in his "Institutes") knows that this truth of total depravity is taught or presupposed on almost every page. One quotation will suffice for our purpose. In it he demonstrates his dependence upon Augustine. In discussing Augustine's use of the term "concupiscence" he writes:

> . . .our nature is not only destitute of all good, but is so fertile in all evils that it cannot remain inactive. Those who have called it *concupiscence* have used an expression not improper, if it were only added, which is far from being conceded by most persons, that everything in man, the understanding and will, the soul and body, is polluted and engrossed by this concupiscence; or, to express it more briefly, that man is of himself nothing else but concupiscence. *(Institutes*, Vol. I, Bk. II, Chap. 1, Para. 8; Allen translation.)

It was this truth which Calvin so sharply set forth as he paid his tribute to Augustine. It was this truth formulated by our fathers at the synod held in Dordrecht.

What then is meant by depravity? What did our fathers mean? What does Scripture teach?

In the first place, depravity has to do, of course, with sin. This seems obvious; yet it is only to the extent that we emphasize the reality and true character of sin that we shall also be able to maintain the truth of total depravity.

Historically and today, those who deny the truth of total depravity are also those who soften the harsh realities of sin. This is why, for example, sin is not taken seriously any more today. Pelagius considered it only a habit. The Semi-pelagians considered it only a sickness. Today also it is easily shrugged off, lightly considered. The horror of sin as it is defined in Scripture is denied. On the far extremes of the ecclesiastical world are the liberal theologians who teach that sin is only a social affliction or a mental deficiency. The cure for sin is to be found then in social rehabilitation, in social do-goodism, in social reform, in outward character reformation. This is the cure for sin because sin is only a remnant of our animal ancestry which we have kept through the upward climb of evoluntionary processes.

But closer to home, to the extent that sin is considered to be only a habit or an illness, the horrible character of sin has been denied and the truth of total depravity has proved impossible to maintain.

Scripture gives us quite a different opinion of sin. Scripture emphatically informs us that sin is always committed in relationship to *God.* That is fundamental. God is the holy, sovereign Lord of heaven and earth. He is infinitely perfect. His holiness is so great and the glory of the brightness of His perfections so brilliant that before Him the angels cover their faces and sing all the day long: "Holy, Holy, Holy is the Lord God Almighty." It is against Him that all sin is committed. This must never be forgotten. Sin is a contradiction of His holiness. It is a rebellion against Him Who is the Lord of heaven and earth. Every sin, no matter how minor, no matter how insignificant, is always committed in relation to God. God created man and set him in Paradise. And the sole purpose of God's creating man was in order that man, who stood at the crown of God's creation, could glorify his Maker. There was not any other purpose why God set man in Paradise than that. With all his life, with all that he was, with all the creation over which he was placed, he had no other calling than to set forth the praise and the glory of God Who alone is worthy of all praise and glory.

Adam's sin of eating of the forbidden tree therefore, was a sin which he committed against God. It was the sin of disobedience against the express command of God. And inasmuch as it was a sin of disobedience against God, it was a deliberate, conscious, wilful determination to cease to perform the purpose for which Adam was created. He wanted nothing to do with God and with His glory any more. He chose to cast his lot with Satan who tempted him. He chose to represent Satan; to aid Satan in Satan's nefarious scheme to steal this world from its Creator. He deliberately turned his back on the God of heaven and earth with that one act of disobedience. That made his sin so horrible. It was committed against God.

To this day, in all the history of this sorry world, there has never been a sin of a different kind. This we must understand. It will never do to talk of sin in terms of social relations, social maladjustment. Sin is against the God of heaven and earth. It is for that reason that the punishment for sin is so very great.

The punishment therefore is that God killed Adam. You can understand why this was necessary. God had formed Adam in order that Adam might represent God's cause in the world, that he might glorify his Maker. He did not have any other purpose for existence than that. He refused to do that. He chose to glorify the devil. That was Adam's desire. But because of this, there was no place for him any more in God's world. So God killed Adam. "The day that thou eatest thereof, thou shalt surely die."

What does that mean, that God killed Adam? He didn't drop dead at the foot of the tree, as we well know. It means, in the first place, that God poured out upon Adam the fury of His wrath and hatred. God hated Adam. It couldn't be any different from this if God was to maintain His own holiness as He always does and must do for His own name's sake. He could not any longer love anyone who sinned and was not holy as He was. You understand that this is now apart from Christ. We know that in Christ Adam was saved. But as far as this death which came upon Adam is concerned, God poured out upon Adam His wrath. It was in the nature of God Himself to do so. Adam was alienated from God. As he was driven out of the garden of Eden, so he was driven from God's face. Where once his life was filled with the sunshine of God's favor, it now was filled with the lowering clouds of God's wrath. Where once he knew peace and joy and happiness and life in fellowship with his Maker, now all that he knew was unrest, alienation, wrath, trouble, affliction, distress, and death.

In the second place, that God killed Adam means that God made Adam totally depraved. That is what death is. Death and total depravity are synonymous. How does the apostle Paul express it in Ephesians 2:1? "But you hath he quickened who were dead in trespasses and sins." The punishment therefore,

15

for Adam's awful transgression was that God brought upon Adam the horror of total depravity. He made him a slave of sin with the whole of his being and nature. That was the punishment for sin. And it is in terms of the punishment for sin that we must consider the truth of total depravity. Because sin is so terrible, it deserves such terrible punishment. That punishment is the total depravity of man's nature. All men therefore are totally depraved.

How is it possible that all men are totally depraved? We must briefly mention two reasons.

In the first place, all men are in Adam responsible for the sin which Adam committed. Because Adam was the head of the whole human race this is true. This is true even as Christ is the Head of His elect people. The apostle Paul expresses that in these words: "For as in Adam all die, even so in Christ shall all be made alive." I Corinthians 15:22. Adam was the head of all men, and all men are therefore responsible with Adam for Adam's transgression.

In the second place, Adam was the father of the whole human race so that from Adam proceeded a human race as corrupt and depraved as he was. It was David who plaintively sang long ago in Psalm 51:5: "Behold, I was shapen in iniquity; and in sin did my mother conceive me."

And so depravity has come upon all men.

II. What Is Meant by *Total* Depravity?

This depravity, Scripture and our Confessions teach us, is total.

Before we enter into a more detailed description of that, I must call your attention to some distinctions that have been made and have become increasingly popular. These distinctions are evidently intended to soften the truth of total depravity. There is, e.g., the distinction which is sometimes made between total depravity and absolute depravity. This distinction is intended to mean that while man is totally depraved, he is not absolutely depraved. The following quotation will serve to elucidate what is meant by this distinction. (It is taken from *The Banner* and is found in an article which is explaining the Canons of Dordt, especially Canons III & IV, Article 4.)

> The result of the fall is total depravity or corruption. By this is meant that every part of man is rendered corrupt. The Canons say that man "became involved in blindness of mind, horrible darkness, vanity, perverseness of judgment; became wicked,

rebellious, obdurate in heart and will and impure in his affection."
There was no part of his nature that was not affected by sin. The
word "total" must not be taken in the absolute sense as though
man is completely depraved. Man is not as bad as he can be.
Article 4, which we hope to consider more fully later in this
series, speaks of "glimmerings of natural light which remain in
man since the fall." God does restrain the working of sin in the
life of man on earth. And sinful man still has a sense of right
and wrong. His corruption is total in the sense that there is no
part of his being that is pure and holy; and the good he does is
done for God and for His glory.

In this quotation the distinction is made between total depravity and absolute depravity. Total depravity means that man is
depraved *in every part of his being*. But while he is depraved in
every part of his being, at the same time there remain in every
part of his being remnants of good. Absolute depravity means
that every part of his being is wholly bad. This distinction therefore is intended precisely to leave room for some good which
man is able to perform. And this good is particularly the good
of accepting with his will the offer of the gospel. That is precisely what our Canons do *not* mean by total depravity.

Another distinction which is oftentimes made is a distinction
between the inward motive of the heart and the outward deed.
There are some who maintain that, while indeed man is, as far
as his nature is concerned, depraved, nevertheless, as far as
his outward deeds are concerned, he is still capable of a considerable amount of good. He can perform works that are exter-
nally in harmony with the law of God. He doesn't live a totally
adulterous life. He doesn't go around shooting his fellow man
with a gun — every man he meets on the street. He is capable of
conforming his life and conduct in an external manner to the law
of God and of performing a great deal of good even though within
he is corrupt.

That too is something which our fathers did not mean. They
spoke of total depravity. And indeed they meant that man is just
as bad as he can be. And this is what Scripture teaches.

There is another distinction which is made between what is
called spiritual good and natural good. The quotation above also
suggests this distinction. By spiritual good is meant good which
is a possible basis for salvation. It is a tentative step in the
direction of heaven. These insist that, while man is indeed incapable of such spiritual good, nevertheless he is definitely
capable of natural good. By natural good is meant something
very much like external goodness which is an external conform-
ity to the law of God. Those who maintain this will point to the

17

world in which we live where much of this natural goodness is to be found.

All of these distinctions, in one way or another, are intended to soften the hardness of the doctrine of total depravity.

When Calvin and the fathers of Dordt insisted that depravity was total, they knew what words mean. And they knew that "total" means precisely that. They intended that the expression *"total* depravity" be a description of what Scripture calls "death". The sinner is dead; spiritually dead. He comes into this world from his mother a spiritual still-born. He is not sick. He is not afflicted with a malady or a disease no matter how fatal. He is dead. And this is the emphatic teaching of Scripture. Always the Scriptures insist that the sinner is dead.

What does this mean?

This means that his nature is so thoroughly corrupted by sin that it is incapable of producing anything good. There is nothing which the sinner can do which is pleasing in the sight of God. His heart is dead. Does not Solomon say, "Out of the heart are all the issues of life?" Prov. 4:23. Yet the heart, the source of all man's life, is dead. Man's mind is dead. It is so darkened by sin that man cannot with his mind know any spiritual good. He can, of course, in a formal sense understand the truth. When a wicked man reads the Scriptures, he can understand what words mean. He can understand the thoughts in these words. This is not the point. But his mind is so thoroughly darkened that every time he sees the truth concerning God he hates it and turns against it. He rebels against its clear teaching. He pushes it away from him. So true is this that Jesus tells Nicodemus (John 3:3): "Except a man be born again, he cannot see the kingdom of God." His mind is so filled with the darkness of the lie that there is no room for the truth in it.

The same is true of man's will. The bondage of the will describes man's state precisely. His will is bound — bound by sin. Man cannot even will the good. The sinner does not, but also cannot will the good. This is his nature. He is dead. Can a dead man think? Can a dead man will? Can a dead man give evidence of life? The spiritually dead man is incapable of any spiritual good.

This is what our Canons express in III & IV, Article 1:

Man was originally formed after the image of God. His understanding was adorned with a true and saving knowledge of his Creator, and of spiritual things; his heart and will were upright; all his affections pure; and the whole man was holy; but

18

revolting from God by the instigation of the devil, and abusing the freedom of his own will, he forfeited these excellent gifts; and on the contrary entailed on himself blindness of mind, horrible darkness, vanity and perverseness of judgment, became wicked, rebellious, and obdurate in heart and will, and impure in his affections.

I cannot think of a worse description of man than that. You object perhaps, and say: "Yes, but the Canons also speak of glimmerings of natural light." This is true. They speak of glimmerings of natural light whereby man retains some knowledge of God, of natural things, and of the differences between good and evil. These glimmerings give man some regard for virtue, for good order in society, and for maintaining an orderly external deportment.

But two points must be made in this connection.

In the first place, when God brought death upon man as the punishment for sin, God did not make man a devil. God did not make man an animal either. Man remained man. And this is what our Canons mean. He was totally depraved; but he was emphatically a totally depraved man. It is sometimes objected that if God had not preserved some remnants of good in man, man would have become a demon or a beast. This is absurd. Man would not have become a demon or a beast if some elements of goodness were not preserved in him. He was created a man. As a man God punishes him. As a man God drives him out of His world. As a man God puts him in hell. But he remains a man. This is what the Canons mean.

In the second place, the Canons explain themselves what these glimmerings of natural light are; and the Canons in the same article (III & IV, 4) show clearly that they do not mean that man is still good.

But so far is this light of nature from being sufficient to bring him to a saving knowledge of God, and to true conversion, that he is incapable of using it aright even in things natural and civil. Nay further, this light, such as it is, man in various ways renders wholly polluted, and holds it in unrighteousness, by doing which he becomes inexcusable before God.

This is the sorry picture of man which our Canons make as they defend the truth of total depravity. And the point is then that if man's nature is dead, one cannot expect that out of that dead nature there will proceed good works. How is this possible? Can a dead man do good? natural good? external good? good by whatever name it is called? Can a rotten tree bring forth good fruit? Can an impure and foul fountain bring forth sweet water? Can a

19

dead corpse bring forth life? If man's nature is depraved, not simply in all of its parts, but in such a way that each part is thoroughly corrupt, then there is no good at all which man can perform in any sense of the word which is pleasing in the sight of God. He cannot do natural good. He cannot do spiritual good. He cannot do civil good. He cannot conform his nature to the law of God. He cannot will his salvation. He is bound hopelessly in the shackles of sin.

Nor must some good be found among the heathen. It is often pictured in our day as if the heathen earnestly crave to be delivered from their idols; earnestly long to escape from the shackles of dark heathendom. And, so it is told us, they would indeed serve the true God if only they knew Who He was. They wait in eager anticipation for someone to tell them about the true God, about Christ, because all their yearnings are in the direction of the true religion. And so it is that when the gospel is preached, this gospel brings to them words which they have long desired to hear; and which now they readily embrace.

But all this can never be. We must not soften the harsh sentence of Scripture. Man is totally depraved. In him is to be found no good thing.

I suppose there are some who would object to all this and insist: "Yes, but when I go out and observe the conduct of my fellow man, I observe something quite contrary to what you say. I see in the world a great deal of love—love between man and wife; love between parents and children; love of man for man. There is a great deal of compassion, philanthropy, desire to help one another in the world of the wicked. There are marvelous accomplishments, which stagger the imagination, on the frontiers of science, technology, and industry. There are wonders of healing performed in medicine. What mighty deeds man can perform! What great things he is capable of! Are not you being unduly harsh? Is not your sentence unjust? Are not you closing your eyes to obvious realities which surround you? Go into the world and you will find that your judgment of man is too severe."

What must we say of this?

There are three points which need to be made.

In the first place, we must be reminded of what was said in the very introduction. We are not formulating the truth of total depravity on the basis of observation. If we do, we shall fail. We must not pay attention to the sentence of man pronounced upon man. We must rather listen to the Word of God — God's sentence upon man. God Who knows the heart. We have one calling, and that is to bow before the Word of God. And God says that man is dead.

In the second place, we must say something about these apparent good deeds.

That problem, strikingly enough, arose already at the time of Augustine. There were those who objected to Augustine's doctrine on the same ground. But Augustine made this very pointed comment: the apparent good which men do is the result of the fact that, in their lives, one kind of lust represses and restrains another kind. He used the example of a man whose whole life is dominated by the lust for money. Such a man is so completely absorbed in acquiring to himself an abundance of material things that this lust is dominant, all-encompassing in his life. It is a completely driving force which banishes all other lusts. In the pursuit of gain, he foregoes all other pleasures. He does not want to squander his money in gluttony, drunkenness, riotous living. He eats sparingly and drinks in moderation. He does not waste his precious hoard of silver and gold in an adulterous life. He thinks this foolish, for he seeks money for its own sake. This is the explanation for the apparent good which men do. One lust restrains another. This was Augustine's answer. And this is true.

Can you call these things the man does "good"? Can you call it good when a man foregoes the pleasures of adultery in order to accumulate for himself greater riches of gold? Is this good in the sight of God? Of course not. The same is true of the so-called apparent philanthropy of men and their many works of mercy. The one driving force in man's life is his lust for honor and recognition. Sin is pride. And man is always attempting to exalt himself before the eyes of his fellow man. In this lustful, dominating drive for honor and fame he is willing to spread his largesse abroad. He is willing to share his riches with his fellow men in order that they may praise him and he may hear, ringing in his ears, the acclaim of those with whom he lives. Is this good? How can it be?

In the broader sense of the word, this is true of the entire history of this sorry world. When God created Adam in Paradise, God set Adam in the midst of this beautiful world only that Adam might love his God with all his heart and mind and soul and strength. He was given the world to glorify his Maker. This was the sole reason for his existence. But Adam refused and bent his ear to the devil. He listened to the devil's whisperings: "You shall be as God, knowing good and evil." Adam took the side of the devil. But it was the devil's purpose -- his unwavering purpose to drive God from His throne and steal this world from God. He enlisted the aid of man to accomplish this. Sin means therefore (from this point of view), that man who stands on the side of the devil, is driven in all that he does to pursue the evil goal of making this world the kingdom of Satan. This determines everything. This is what sin is all about. It is hatred of God. It is rebellion against the Most High. And it is,therefore, a desperate, undying attempt on the part of man to seize this world in which he has been placed and make it his own; to drive God out of His world; to depose Christ from His throne; to make this universe subservient to the cause of sin. And, in order to accomplish that goal, he is willing to bend every effort at his disposal. He is willing to use every means available. And if he must, in the pursuit of this goal, forego for a little while certain other pleasures in order to accomplish this, he is willing to do it. He knows then that if government is not instituted to make laws and enforce them, anarchy will prevail. And anarchy will prevent him from attaining his goals. And so he not only makes laws, but also conforms his life to them. That is, he will do this as long as is necessary to drive God out of His world. Just as soon as he believes he can safely escape the fury of God's wrath, the consequences of sin, he will do as he pleases. He will sit back in his pride and say: "The world is mine. God is gone. I can do as I please -- sin all I want. There is no need any more of bearing sin's consequences. God is banished from His throne." Everything man does, therefore, (all this apparent good) is determined by this overriding desire. He may stand on the frontiers of space. He may make marvelous inventions in the fields of science. But it is because he is engaged in a desperate struggle to wrench this world from the hands of the Creator. He will not rest until that goal is reached. This is the deepest principle of his life. This is why all the human race's sin culminates at last in that man of sin, the Son of Perdition, Antichrist. In Antichrist he thinks he has attained his goal.

Indeed man's depravity is *total.*

III. What Is The Importance Of This Doctrine?

There are two remarks which we must make by way of conclusion.

In the first place, the importance of this doctrine is theological.

This means two things.

First of all, the truth of total depravity is not an isolated doctrine. It is closely connected to and interwoven with the

22

other four points of Calvinism. And because this is true, this doctrine is closely connected with the whole truth of Scripture. It is with good reason that our beautiful Heidelberg Catechism begins its entire discussion of the truth with the significant statement of total depravity:

Are we then so corrupt that we are wholly incapable of doing any good, and inclined to all wickedness?

Indeed we are; except we are regenerated by the Spirit of God.

It is on this foundation that the Catechism erects the whole structure of the truth. The truth of total depravity is part of the whole truth of Scripture. If this truth is denied, softened, vitiated in any respect, it becomes impossible to preserve any of the truth of God's Word. Historically this has proved true. And this lies in the nature of the case. And so this is true also of the five points of Calvinism. A denial of total depravity leads to a denial of sovereign grace. This in turn leads to a denial of limited atonement and unconditional election. And the preservation of the saints necessarily falls by the wayside. This cannot be demonstrated in detail in this chapter. This shall be amply made clear in the chapters to follow. But it ought to be clear that if man is not totally depraved, then grace cannot possibly be sovereign. To the extent that he is not totally depraved, he is capable of doing good. And to that extent he is capable of participating in the work of salvation. And to that extent grace is not sovereign at all. The two truths stand or fall together. And so it is with the whole of the truth.

Secondly, all this means (and this is most serious) that the truth of total depravity is the only truth which preserves intact the glory of God. To the extent that good is ascribed to man, glory is taken away from the only adorable God. To the extent that man is said to be other than the awful sentence of Scripture, God is no more the glorious sovereign and holy God of heaven and earth.

And this brings us to the last point. This truth is also important as far as the life of the child of God is concerned.

The doctrine of total depravity is not cold and abstract dogma. It is the living confession of the people of God. But even that confession is not something which they make of themselves. It is the fruit of grace. For characteristic of the sinner is that he exalts himself in pride, haughtiness and arrogance. In his frightening conceit he refuses to admit his total depravity and boasts of his own goodness before the face of the Most High. But when the shining light of God's holiness and the sovereign power of grace penetrates into the heart of God's elect child, and he sees himself standing exposed before the face of Him Who searches the hearts, then he hears thundering in his ears the awful sentence of Scripture. He sees himself as worthless, corrupt, depraved, incapable of doing any good. And the words of the saints of all ages ring in his own heart: "Behold, I was shapen in iniquity; and in sin did my mother conceive me." "God be merciful to me, a sinner." "Oh, wretched man that I am. Who shall deliver me from the body of this death?"

This is the living confession of the child of God. And when that confession grips his soul and he sees himself as he truly is, as God's Word describes him, then, with tear-filled eyes, he can also see the cross. Only then. For in the consciousness of sin he can see the wonder, the power of the cross; the mercy and grace revealed there; the infinite splendor and love of God manifested in that blood-spattered tree. And seeing this, he sees the wonder of sovereign grace; and from his heart arises a doxology of praise and glory to God – the God of his salvation.

Chapter II

Unconditional Election

Unconditional Election

Herman Hanko

The following is a statement of the doctrine of divine predestination:

> That God, by an eternal, unchangeable purpose in Jesus Christ His Son, before the foundation of the world, hath determined, out of a fallen, sinful race of men, to save in Christ, for Christ's sake, and through Christ, those who, through the grace of the Holy Spirit, shall believe on this his Son Jesus, and shall persevere in this faith and obedience of faith, through this grace, even to the end; and, on the other hand, to leave the incorrigible and unbelieving in sin and under wrath, and to condemn them as alienate from Christ, according to the word of the gospel in John 3:36: "He that believeth on the Son hath everlasting life: and he that believeth not the Son shall not see life; but the wrath of God abideth on him," and according to other passages of Scripture also.

It might be of considerable interest to ask our readers whether they consider this particular description of predestination an acceptable definition of the doctrine. Indeed, if even some of them find this definition acceptable and precise according to the Scriptures, it would only be an eloquent testimony of the fact that the doctrine of election is all but foreign to the Reformed Church world of today. The fact of the matter is that this quotation is the first point composed by the Arminians in the first part of the 17th Century, which along with four other points of doctrine, the Arminians submitted to the Reformed Churches of the Low Countries for their consideration and approval. And when our fathers considered this statement concerning the doctrine of election, they rejected it as being emphatically heretical; and composed as an answer to it the first chapter of our Canons of Dordrecht.

Some might ask the question: What is so bad about this statement? Is it not conceivable perhaps that our fathers and the Reformed Churches who rejected this statement were being picayune, concerning themselves with minor and insignificant details? Is it not after all, an acceptable definition of the doctrine of election on the basis of which we all can stand? The answer of our fathers was a most emphatic and vehement "No!" That ought to be our answer as well.

If we quote once again the key statement of this definition, perhaps the error of it will be clarified:

That God hath determined to save in Christ, those who shall believe on this His Son Jesus, and shall persevere in this faith and obedience of faith even to the end.

That is particularly the phrase to which our fathers objected. The objection was that, although this statement of the Arminians is couched in Reformed and apparently Scriptural language, nevertheless it is an introduction into the faith of the Reformed Churches of the doctrine of *conditional* election: election based upon foreseen faith and perseverance in faith. And our fathers insisted, over against this statement, that the truth of Scripture, of the Reformed Confessions and of the Reformed Churches since the time of the Protestant Reformation was the truth of unconditional election.

This truth is the subject of this chapter.

It is apparent that all the five points of Calvinism with which this booklet has to do are important. Indeed, if any one of the five points of Calvinism is denied, the Reformed heritage is completely lost. But it is certain that the truth of unconditional election stands at the foundation of them all. This truth is the touchstone of the Reformed faith. It is the basis of the truth of God concerning our salvation. It is the very heart and core of the gospel. It is the basis of all the comfort and assurance of the people of God in the midst of the world. It alone inspires in the hearts of the faithful the burning hope of life everlasting. No doubt it is precisely for this reason that no other single truth in all the history of the church has been so viciously and consistently attacked as the truth of unconditional election. But no man can claim ever to be either Calvinistic or Reformed without a firm and abiding commitment to this precious truth.

We discuss this truth under the following three questions which we shall ask and answer:

I. What Is Meant By Unconditional Election?
II. What Are The Denials Of This Truth?
III. What Is Its Importance For The Church?

I. What Is Meant By Unconditional Election?

Before we proceed to define what is meant by unconditional election, it is important to recall briefly the history of this truth

28

in the church. We are generally accustomed to trace this truth of unconditional election back to the Calvin Reformation. And yet it was not Calvin who was the first to develop this truth. But, just as with the truth of total depravity, so also with this truth, St. Augustine, who lived more than a millennium ago in the Fifth Century A.D., was the first to speak of it. If we consider this a moment, this is not surprising. Augustine took the position that man is totally depraved. By this he meant that man is incapable of doing any good. And, most emphatically, that man is incapable of doing anything which would contribute to his salvation. In answer, therefore, to the question of how men are saved, Augustine answered that the power of salvation is to be found only in the power of sovereign, unmerited grace. There is no other power of salvation but that. But immediately the question arises: If the power of salvation is the power of sovereign, unmerited grace, not dependent in any respect upon man, how is it then that some men are saved and others are not? The answer to that question Augustine found in the decree of election and reprobation. He developed this truth therefore as part of his answer to the error of Pelagianism.

Sad to say, this truth was never officially accepted by the Roman Catholic Church in the form which Augustine gave to it. Even though Rome honors Augustine as a church father, his doctrines were soon lost. In the dreary ages between Augustine and John Calvin there could be found only very few who maintained this truth with the emphasis that Augustine placed upon it. One such man was Gottschalk, a German theologian, who, having read Augustine, became convinced of the truth of sovereign predestination. But he was imprisoned for teaching it and paid the ultimate price of a martyr's death, rotting in some foul dungeon in France, sentenced there by the Church.

It was not therefore until the time of the Protestant Reformation that the truth of sovereign predestination was brought to the fore. Luther believed it, maintained it, and taught it with emphasis. But Luther never made it an integral part of his theology. Luther's chief concern was the truth of justification by faith; and he never developed this truth of sovereign predestination in all its Scriptural emphases.

This work was done by John Calvin. And, indeed, if there was one reason why Calvin was hated it was because he maintained so unswervingly the truth of unconditional election.

This truth therefore became an important part of the confession of all the churches which follow the theology of the reformer of Geneva. The truth of unconditional election is incorporated into the Confessions of all the Reformed and Calvinistic Churches not only in Europe, but also in this country.

It was in the latter part of the century of the Reformation and the early part of the 17th Century that this truth was attacked by Arminius. He was professor of theology in the Reformed University of Leyden, had studied in Geneva at the Academy, but nevertheless openly repudiated the truth of predestination. But, as so often happens when heresy is introduced into the church of Christ, so in this case also, Arminius and those who supported him attempted to bring their teaching into the church under the banner of the Reformed faith. They tried to pass off their heresy as the teaching of Scripture, claiming that this ought to be the confession of the Reformed Churches. But our fathers would have none of this and pointed out in no uncertain language that the conditional election of the Arminians was not the truth of Scripture nor the heritage of the Calvinistic and Reformed Reformation.

It is not difficult to understand why the Arminians taught conditional election. They did not believe in total depravity to begin with. They wanted to preserve in man the freedom of his will — the power of man's will to choose for the good, to accept the offer of the gospel. It was their contention that God on His part loved all men, that hatred and wrath were foreign to God's nature; that it was God's intention and desire to save all men; that, therefore, God made salvation available and obtainable to all men through the universal atonement — a universal cross on which Christ died for the sins of every man. But it is clear that in such a system as that proposed by the Arminians, there is no room at all for unconditional election. While therefore, the Arminians wanted to retain Reformed and Scriptural language and speak of election, they cut the heart out of this important and beautiful truth by insisting that election is conditional. God elects those whom He knows will believe, the Arminians said. God elects those whom He knows will accept the gospel which is offered to them. God elects those whom He knows will, by an act of their will, accept the gospel and who will also persevere in that acceptance of the gospel and keep that faith which once they exercised. Election is based upon this work of man.

But it was precisely this description of the truth of election which our fathers strenuously opposed. They saw it not as a minor point, not as an insignificant detail of the truth for which there was room in the Reformed Churches. They saw it as a threat to the truth, as a teaching which cut the heart out of the whole truth of God's Word. They saw that it destroyed the truth of God's work of salvation as taught in Scripture. And they insisted therefore, that election is unconditional.

What is meant by election?

There are several words used in Scripture to define this truth. The word "election" itself is used in Romans 9:11:

> For the children being not yet born, neither having done any good or evil, that the purpose of God according to election might stand, not of works, but of him that calleth; It was said unto her, The elder shall serve the younger.

The other two words -- "to foreknow" and "to predestinate" -- are both used in Romans 8:29:

> For whom he did foreknow, he also did predestinate to be conformed to the image of his Son, that he might be the firstborn among many brethren. Moreover whom He did predestinate, them he also called: and whom he called, them he also justified: and whom he justified, them he also glorified.

When the Scriptures speak of election it is evident that this refers to the counsel of God. In Eph. 1 the apostle Paul describes election in these words:

> Blessed be the God and Father of our Lord Jesus Christ, who hath blessed us with all spiritual blessings in heavenly places in Christ: According as he hath chosen us in him before the foundation of the world, that we should be holy and without blame before him . . . having made known unto us the mystery of his will, according to his good pleasure which he hath purposed in himself: . . . In whom (Christ) also we have obtained an inheritance, being predestinated according to the purpose of him who worketh all things after the counsel of his own will. (vss. 3, 4, 9, 11.)

If, therefore, we are to understand the truth of election, we must discuss briefly the truth of the counsel of God. There is no room to discuss this important truth in detail, but some remarks must be made.

In the first place, it is important to notice that God's counsel cannot be compared with a plan — as so often it is. We speak of God's counsel as a plan; but it is possible that when we use this terminology we have in our minds something like the plan of an architect who makes a drawing of a proposed building. God's counsel is not that kind of plan. It is not written on a piece of paper and filed away somewhere in heaven. Nor is God's counsel even some kind of plan which is similar to a proposed course of action which we have in our minds. If we intend to go on a trip, e.g., we make our plans for that trip. But this is not the way we must consider the counsel of God.

Rather, God's counsel is His own living will. It is the living will of the God of heaven and earth. That is a fundamental truth from which all the rest of the truth of God's counsel necessarily follows. To deny this truth is really to deny the counsel of God altogether.

In the second place, God's counsel is eternal. The will of God is the will of the *eternal* God. If God is eternal and His will is eternal, His counsel is equally eternal. This means, in brief, that God is never without His counsel. The creation and the world have a beginning. God does not. He is above time, untouched by time's passing moments, dwelling in the serenity of eternity. What is true of God is true of His counsel.

In the third place, because God's counsel is His living will, God's counsel is also absolutely unchangeable. "I am Jehovah," the prophet Malachi informs Israel, "I change not. Therefore ye sons of Jacob are not consumed." (3:6) The unchangeableness of God's own being is also the unchangeableness of His eternal counsel. There is nothing which can alter His counsel; nothing which can force God to revise it in any respect; nothing which can introduce into God's counsel alteration or amendment. It is eternal and unchangeable. We use the expression sometimes: "Prayer changes things." It is not clear what is meant by this vague and ambiguous expression. But if the meaning is that by means of our prayers the will and counsel of God is altered, that He does not do what He originally determined to do, then this expression must be condemned. There is nothing which can or does change the counsel of God.

In the fourth place, because that counsel of God is His living will, it is sovereignly efficacious. All that God has determined to do in His counsel will also be done. No power can frustrate it. All power belongs to God. No contingencies of life can prevent it from being realized. Everything that God has determined to do in His eternal and unchangeable counsel will certainly come to pass with absolute precision as He has determined it before the foundations of the world.

In the fifth place, the purpose of God's counsel — the reason why He made His counsel, is the glory of his own name. God determined to glorify Himself. Not because He needed this glory to make His life as He lives it in Himself perfect. Not because His glory is incomplete. Not because, in any respect, the things which He determined to do in His counsel will make His glory richer and fuller than it is. But simply because He chose to reveal the glory of His own being in order that His glory might

32

be acknowledged. All that God does, therefore, is determined by God's glory which He seeks.

But God, according to the Scriptures, desires to glorify Himself through Christ. This is the whole thrust of that beautiful passage in Ephesians 1 which speaks of election. God determines to make His glory known -- but through Christ. That is, through Christ as He is born of a virgin and lived among us; through Christ as He suffers and dies on the cross; through Christ as He rises in power and glory from the dead; through Christ as He is exalted in the highest heavens; through Christ as He shall come again at the end of time to establish the everlasting kingdom of righteousness; through that Christ God reveals all the glory of His own divine being. Christ is the fulness of the revelation of the glory of God.

It is this which brings us to the heart of our subject because just as soon as we say "Christ," we also say "the elect." There is no Christ apart from the elect. He was born in Bethlehem, but He came into our flesh. He died on the cross in the place of His people to satisfy the justice of God which demanded punishment for sin. He arose again from the grave of His people to conquer death on their behalf. He is in heaven at God's right hand to pray for His people and to prepare all things that His people may come to Him in everlasting glory. And all this is true because the elect are chosen in Christ from before the foundation of the world. God, inasmuch as He determines to glorify Himself in Christ, determines to glorify Himself in an elect people whom He chooses in Christ and who are destined to dwell with Christ forever in everlasting life.

This is the truth of God's counsel. All that we have said concerning God's counsel, therefore, must equally be said concerning predestination -- both election and reprobation.

Election is, therefore, that decree of God which He eternally makes, by which, with sovereign freedom, He chooses to Himself a people, upon whom He determines to set His love, whom He rescues from sin and death through Jesus Christ, unto Himself in everlasting glory.

This election is sovereign — God's sovereign and free choice. This election is eternal even as God's counsel is eternal. This election is unchangeable even as God's counsel is unchangeable. This election is efficacious so that the decree of election itself is, through Christ, the power by which the elect are actually saved.

Election is therefore definite and particular. Perhaps this

needs emphasis. There are some who maintain that election is a general choice on the part of God so that He only decides to save some people. But just exactly who those people are whom God has decided to save is not decided by the decree of election. This is, once again, the old familiar Arminian ploy. It is only decided that God will save some; but precisely whom He will save is decided on the basis of what man himself will do with the offer of the gospel. This is not election -- either of Scripture or the Reformed heritage. God knows His own from before the foundation of the world and chooses them, knowing their names and penning their names on the pages of the Book of Life. So that each one stands before God's mind and heart eternally as the object of His love.

Now this election is unconditional. We believe in unconditional election. And it is this truth of unconditional election which must be maintained because it stands overagainst the Arminian heresy which teaches that election is conditional.

Once again, it ought to be clear that this truth of unconditional election is not merely a subtle distinction, a minor and insignificant detail. When our fathers insisted upon this truth, they were not interested in splitting hairs -- as they have so often been accused of doing. The Arminians were destroying the whole work of God in salvation when they proposed their heresy. You may be sure that the same is true today. It is cruelly unjust to accuse those who maintain the truth of unconditional election of being guilty of fastening on insignificant details of the truth. The fact is that unless we maintain unconditional election, there is no election at all. By making election conditional the heart is cut from the truth of salvation, because then the power of sovereign grace is denied as the power by which God saves those whom He has chosen to be His own. Then limited atonement is denied even though this truth is taught on every page of Scripture. Then total depravity is denied and many good things are found in man, chief of which is his ability to assist in the work of salvation. It is conditional election which paves the way for all these other heresies. It all fits in. For then God's choice is not sovereign, but is dependent upon what man will do with the salvation which God lovingly offers to him, but which will not be his unless he receives it by his own power to accept or reject it.

It might not be amiss to notice somewhat in passing, that the position of the Arminians is extremely involved and complicated. It is difficult, to say the least, to understand the Arminian position. Many questions arise which the Arminians themselves have chosen not to answer, but which they shrug off with the convenient excuse that these are "apparent contradictions". For example, if God desires to save all men, and yet all men are not saved, is not the purpose of God frustrated by man? Is not the almighty sovereign of heaven and earth overcome by the puny strength of man? The inevitable answer to this embarrassing question is: This is an apparent contradiction which we cannot explain. But surely, overagainst this complicated and involved position of the Arminians, the truth of Scripture is clear and easy to understand. Whether men agree with it or not is, after all, not the question. But men can understand it. It is simple enough for a child to understand. It avoids all the pitfalls and embarrassing questions of the position of Arminianism.

But however this may be, it is the truth of unconditional election which we must maintain. What does this mean?

First of all (and negatively) this means that in the decrees of election God chose *not* according to anything found in man. He did not base His choice on man in any way. Not on man's goodness, works, faith, holiness; not on man's faithfulness to the gospel. There could not be found in man any good thing. It was a free choice, a sovereign choice of God. He made it without any consideration of man whatsoever. The apostle Paul expresses this in Romans 9:10-13. Paul is speaking of Jacob and Esau — children of Isaac and Rebecca. He writes:

> And not only this; but when Rebecca also had conceived by one, even by our father Isaac; (For the children being not yet born, neither having done any good or evil, that the purpose of God according to election might stand, not of works, but of him that calleth;) It was said unto her, The elder shall serve the younger. As it is written, Jacob have I loved, but Esau have I hated.

This same truth was expressed in the Old Dispensation when Israel was brought to the borders of Canaan. God told Israel through Moses:

> The Lord did not set his love upon you, nor choose you, because ye were more in number than any people; for you were the fewest of all people: But because the Lord loved you, and because he would keep the oath which he had sworn unto your fathers, hath the Lord brought you out with a mighty hand, and redeemed you out of the house of bondage, from the hand of Pharaoh king of Egypt. (Deut. 7:7, 8.)

The choice of God was not because Israel had any distinctive traits about her which set her apart from the other nations. The only reason why God chose Israel was because God loved her. His choice was free and sovereign.

Secondly, and positively, that election is based solely upon God's good pleasure. In Ephesians 1:4ff. the truth of this is set forth.

> According as he hath chosen us in him before the foundation of the world, that we should be holy and without blame before him in love: Having predestinated us unto the adoption of children by Jesus Christ to himself according to the good pleasure of his will.

This is the only basis for election. God chose those whom He chose because it seemed good to Him to do it. It was His good pleasure. It was the good pleasure of His own eternal and unchangeable will. It was His because He had determined to glorify Himself in His own way through a people whom He would choose.

Thirdly, this means that all the blessings of salvation flow forth from the decree of election. We are not chosen because we believe, but rather because God is pleased to choose us. And faith and perseverance in faith are blessings which come to us through election. Election is the fountain of every good work. Our Canons (quite expectedly) emphasize this very strongly.

> That some receive the gift of faith from God, and others do not receive it proceeds from God's eternal decree. . . . (I, 6.)

> This election was not founded upon foreseen faith, and the obedience of faith, holiness, or any other good quality or disposition in man, as the pre-requisite, cause or condition on which it depended, but men are chosen to faith and to the obedience of faith, holiness, etc., therefore election is the fountain of every saving good, from which proceed faith, holiness, and the other gifts of salvation, and finally eternal life itself, as its fruits and effects . . . . (I, 9.)

In this connection, a word must also be said concerning the truth of reprobation, although space forbids us to enter into this in detail.

In the first place, it must be emphasized that the truth of election and reprobation stand or fall together. To deny election is to deny reprobation. To deny reprobation is to deny election. To believe election is to believe reprobation. To believe reprobation is to believe election. There is no compromise at this point. Calvin has a very beautiful quote concerning this in his *Institutes*. He writes in Bk. III, Chap. XXIII, Para. 1:

> Many, indeed, as if they wished to avert odium from God, admit election in such a way as to deny that any one is reprobated. But this is puerile and absurd, because election itself could not exist without being opposed to reprobation. God is said

to separate those whom he adopts to salvation. Whom God passes by, therefore, he reprobates, and from no other cause than his determination to exclude them from the inheritance which he predestines for his children. And the petulance of men is intolerable, if it refuses to be restrained by the word of God, which treats of his incomprehensible counsel, adored by angels themselves.

This is Calvinism and the Reformed faith.

In the second place, God's decree of reprobation is also a decree of His sovereign, eternal and unchangeable counsel. According to that decree God determined to reveal His justice, wrath, and hatred of sin, and in this way the holiness of His own divine being, in vessels of wrath fitted for destruction and punished everlastingly in hell because of their sins.

This is the truth of reprobation.

II. What Are The Denials Of This Truth?

It is not at all strange that this truth of predestination is denied almost universally. The sad part of it is that it is denied also by those who sail under the Reformed flag and claim to be Calvinists. This is deceit.

There are many ways in which this truth is denied.

We have already discussed the denial of Arminianism. Today it is evident that those who adopt the position of Arminians do not speak of predestination at all any more. It is lost. Principally Arminianism has no room for predestination.

There are others who deny this truth simply by being quiet about it. This is perhaps more common than any other form of denial within Reformed circles. They say they believe it. But they very pointedly omit it from all their preaching and teaching and writing. The idea is, of course, to kill it with silence. That, too, is a denial of predestination. The justification for this silence is supposed to be that predestination belongs to the hidden things of God. It is claimed that predestination belongs to those hidden things of God while we have to do only with that which is revealed to us and to our children. Therefore, while these who make this claim, insist that they believe this doctrine of predestination, they are silent about it because they claim that by speaking of it they pry into secret things which are not their concern. But all this is simply not true. While indeed God has not revealed specifically *who* each one of His elect are, nevertheless the truth of election itself is found on every page of Scripture. Turn where you will and, if it is not explicitly stated, it is nevertheless presupposed. And because this truth is revealed so clearly, it must also be the confession of the people of God.

There are others who deny election forthrightly. This is not only true among the modernists; this is true also in Reformed circles. The following quote is taken from *The Reformed Journal,* the issue of January, 1967 as an example of this.

> What about God's reprobation or rejection? Does not election *logically imply* rejection? . . . Does not election really mean selection? . . . Israel's election, though sometimes misunderstood by the people themselves, ultimately meant their being called for service to the other nations. Therefore it was not a case of the other nations being forever excluded, but of God's electing Israel *on his way to the others.* Election in the biblical sense does imply service, but apparently it does *not* imply rejection . . . .

There are two main points which the author is making here. In the first place, the author is saying that election is not that God eternally, unchangeably determined in Christ who would be His people destined to live with Him forever in heaven. But rather election means only that God took the nation of Israel as a nation and set it aside so that it could be responsible for bringing the gospel to the whole world. This is all election means according to this article.

In the second place, because the nation of Israel is chosen to be the vehicle by which God brings the gospel to the whole world, there is no such thing as reprobation or rejection, for the whole world is elect in Israel. And in this way the author supports what he considers to be the truth of universal atonement and the universal love of God.

This is a forthright denial of the truth of election and reprobation. It remains a mystery how this can appear under the name of "Reformed".

There are others who deny the truth of predestination by raising objections against the doctrine. These objections are as old as the doctrine is. The same objections we hear today were raised already in the days of Augustine -- indeed, in the days of the apostle Paul. If we examine these objections they come down to two main ones.

In the first place there is a class of objections against this doctrine which contains charges against God Himself. The objection is raised that predestination makes God a tyrant, the author of sin, a capricious dictator who arbitrarily chooses some and rejects others.   They are similar to the objections which Paul considered in Romans 9:14, 19:

What shall we say then? Is there unrighteousness with God?

Thou wilt say then unto me, Why doth he yet find fault? For who hath resisted his will?

They are objections lodged against God and His justice.

The other class of objections all come down to the one charge of fatalism. It is said that the truth of predestination is fatalistic and that it is similar to the horrible doctrine of the Moham- medans.   These objections mean to say that the truth of predest- ination makes of men careless and profane sinners. The doctrine arouses in men the statement: "Let us sin that grace may abound."   The doctrine forces men to say: "If I'm an elect, I am going to heaven no matter what I do -- even though I sin greatly. So I shall have a good time in this life, for my sin cannot alter my election.   And, on the other hand, if I am not an elect, I will not go to heaven no matter how good a life I live. Hence I shall surely go to hell if I am reprobate even though I live holily. So I might just as well enjoy life, sin as much as possible. Nothing can alter God's eternal determination." So, it is said, the doctrine of predestination destroys man's responsibility and accountability, and makes of him a stock and a block.

All these objections are very old.

What shall we answer?

In the first place, in general, there are times when these questions are raised by sincere people of God. They are not raised in order to make mockery of the truth; but rather because the people of God want to understand the truth as clearly as they are able. And then these questions are perfectly legitimate.

But most of the time these objections are made by evil men who hate this truth. They are raised to slander the truth, to make the doctrine odious in the minds of men, to try to persuade men to discard the doctrine.   Almost always these are objections which arise from evil hearts and not from the humble question- ings of the people of God.

It is well to remember this, because if evil is the motive, nothing Scripture says will alter these objections in any way.

In the second place, we must be prepared to admit that this truth is very profound.   There are indeed questions which will arise in our minds which we shall be unable to answer. Calvin, for example, reminds us again and again that we must limit ourselves to what Scripture says and not permit ourselves to wander beyond the paths in which Scripture leads us. Where Scripture tells us to stop, there we must stop. And, if at that stopping point, there are still questions that are unanswered, so be it; we bow in humility before the truth of the Word of God. However, this truth is sometimes used to deny the truth of predestination in a very subtle way and to block the investigation of this truth altogether. And so it must be emphasized that although we may not go into paths where Scripture does not lead us, we must follow where Scripture takes us by the hand and shows us the glory of this work of God. When Scripture puts this confession on our lips, this confession must be ours.

In the third place, with respect to the first class of objections (charging God with capriciousness and making Him the author of sin) we can do no better than quote the answer of Paul to similar objections:

> What shall we say then? Is there unrighteousness with God? God forbid. For he saith to Moses, I will have mercy on whom I will have mercy, and I will have compassion on whom I will have compassion. So then it is not of him that willeth, nor of him that runneth, but of God that sheweth mercy. For the scripture saith unto Pharaoh, Even for this same purpose have I raised thee up, that I mighty shew my power in thee, and that my name might be declared throughout all the earth. Therefore hath he mercy on whom he will have mercy, and whom he will he hardeneth. Thou wilt say then unto me, Why doth he yet find fault? For who hath resisted his will? Nay but, O man, who art thou that repliest against God? Shall the thing formed say to him that formed it, Why hast thou made me thus? Hath not the potter power over the clay, of the same lump to make one vessel unto honour, and another unto dishonour? (Romans 9:14-21)

That is the answer of Scripture; that must be our answer too.

Finally, with respect to charges of fatalism, every child of God knows in his heart that they are not true. The history of the Reformed Churches is abundant testimony that it is not true. Is not this history written in the blood of martyrs who loved not their lives unto death because they believed and confessed the truth of eternal election? Is there not a long gallery of heroes of faith who loved this truth and confessed it and whose lives are a testimony of the power of God's grace in their hearts?

There is reason for this. For the truth of election not only means that God chooses those who are to be His people; and it not only means that God determines that they shall live in heaven; but it means also that God guarantees a walk of holiness for His people in the midst of the world. The decree of election is the foundation of all the blessings of salvation. Election was realized on Calvary. And on Calvary all of salvation was accomplished. That same salvation is applied to the hearts of God's elect people by sovereign grace. This is the point our Canons make again and again.

> There are not various decrees of election, but one and the same decree respecting all those, who shall be saved, both under the Old and New Testament: since the scripture declares the good pleasure, purpose and counsel of the divine will to be one, according to which he hath chosen us from eternity, both to grace and glory, *to salvation and the way of salvation, which he hath ordained that we should walk therein.* (I, 8; italics added.) Cf. also I, 6, 9, quoted above.

Election is the fountain of an innumerable host of blessings which flow to God's people. By the power of this election they walk as God's people in the midst of the world. Careless and profane Christians? No. Elect, redeemed in the blood of the cross and sanctified by the power of sovereign grace.

III. What Is Its Importance For The Church?

The importance of this doctrine is to be found first of all in its theological significance. It is the central truth of all the Scriptures. While it is literally taught in hundreds of places in God's Word, it is also the underlying truth upon which the whole of Scripture as the revelation of God in Christ is based. It is present in every passage, presupposed in every part, an integral truth of the whole of God's revelation. And this is because Scripture is the revelation of God Who saves. God is sovereign. All glory belongs to Him alone. It is this truth which raises our hearts to a contemplation of the adorable God of heaven and earth and prostrates us in adoration before Him.

Holding this truth, therefore, the whole Scripture is a beautiful unity. There is no need for abstruse distinctions. There is no need to follow a double-track theology. It is all a beautiful whole. God is sovereign in the choice of His people. And as the sovereign, He redeems in the cross those whom He has chosen. As the sovereign He places His love upon His people and He hates the wicked all the day. As the sovereign He shows favor through the cross to those who belong to Him; but pours out His wrath upon all the workers of iniquity. His grace also, therefore, is never common. It is always particular — bestowed through the cross upon the objects of His choice. And it is irresistible in its particularity because those whom He chooses shall surely be brought to final salvation and blessedness.

The choice therefore is either - or. We may deny this truth, but then we must also make God a helpless god, fashioned after our thoughts, dependent upon the fickle will of man, working only after man makes his choices and decisions, altering His plan according to man's whims, dependent upon man's final work. Or we make our choice for the truth of Scripture and maintain the truth of a great and sovereign God of heaven and earth to Whom alone belongs all praise and glory forever.

Thus this doctrine of election, in the second place, affords the people of God unspeakable consolation. We are only sinners who add daily to the burden of our guilt. If salvation were left to us, we would be tossed about on the stormy seas of doubt. We can merit nothing with God. But election, sovereign election, is an immoveable rock upon which we stand; and, standing, are safe from all harm. The elect can never perish. "Nevertheless the foundation of God standeth sure, having this seal, The Lord knoweth them that are his. And, Let every one that nameth the name of Christ depart from iniquity." II Tim. 2:19. God will preserve the work of grace in the hearts of His own until the end.

We can do no better than to close this discussion with the words Paul uses to close his discussion of this truth. They are found in Romans 11:33-36:

O the depth of the riches both of the wisdom and knowledge of God! how unsearchable are his judgments, and his ways past finding out! For who hath known the mind of the Lord? or who hath been his counsellor? Or who hath first given to him, and it shall be recompensed again? For of him, and through him, and to him, are all things: to whom be glory forever. Amen.

Chapter III

Limited Atonement

Limited Atonement

Homer C. Hoeksema

Nowadays when you hear the expression "Limited Atonement" you immediately think of the debate and, to an extent, controversy that is going on in the Reformed community exactly about this subject. And if you expect that in this chapter I will have something to say about matters connected with what generally has come to be called the "Dekker Case," you are correct.

But I wish to make the following crystal clear in this connection.

In the first place, I have absolutely no interest in and no intention of engaging in personalities or in tearing down or railing against anyone's church, whatever the name of that church may be, or in gloating about anyone's ecclesiastical difficulties. I want no part of that. The matter of the church and the matter of the truth of our Reformed heritage are far too serious for that. Let this, therefore, be understood.

In the second place, the other side of the previous statement is that I am interested solely in the truth of the gospel and its advance; and I approach you, my readers, on that same basis. I expect that you are interested in the same thing. And let me add immediately that for me the truth of the gospel and the Reformed faith are *synonymous*.

In the third place the question is, therefore, solely this: what do our Reformed confessions say about this doctrine, and what does Scripture, on which our Reformed confessions are based, say about it? That is the only issue. The issue is not one of theological opinions. Nor is it a question of what is popular, — because certainly the Reformed truth is not very popular today. Nor is it a question of what is apparently useful or what may apparently be harmful in the preaching or on the mission field. Nor is it a question of what we would like to think. But the issue, first of all, for Reformed believers is this: what do our confessions, which we agree are binding and to which Reformed officebearers must subscribe, — what do these confessions say?

To this, if we are Reformed, we must agree. If we do not, then we should be honest enough to say, "I don't want to be Reformed." And ultimately, of course, the issue is one of Scripture. Before Scripture, whatever it says, you and I have no choice but to bow.

In the fourth place, I do not intend to develop this subject negatively: I do not like to be negative. I wish to develop, ᵧ as much as possible in the course of this one chapter, -- the Reformed and Scriptural truth concerning the atonement *positively,* in order then to point out the negative implications with respect to various departures from that truth.

In the fifth place, I hope you will understand that I must needs limit myself to trying to sketch the main lines and the main implications of this very rich truth. Undoubtedly several chapters could easily be devoted to this one subject; and this would also be worthwhile. But that is not our purpose now; it is not our purpose to go into all the details of this subject. We are rather interested in the main lines of this so-called Third Point of Calvinism. These main lines I wish to sketch, taking for granted that you have followed the exposition already made by my colleague, Professor Hanko, in the two previous chapters, as well as in the expectation that you will follow the further implications of this doctrine of the atonement as they shall be expounded by Pastor Van Baren in the fourth and fifth chapters of this booklet.

Finally, -- by way of introduction, -- I had intended to devote one entire point of this lecture to the subject of the relative importance of this truth of Limited Atonement in the whole of the Five Points of Calvinism and in the whole of the truth of salvation by grace. This, however, would unduly lengthen this chapter. But I want to point out by way of introduction, first of all, that it is in this truth of limited atonement that the doctrine of sovereign election (and, in fact, sovereign predestination with its two aspects of election and reprobation) comes into focus. The cross is the objective realization and revelation of God's predestinating purpose. That revelation of God's sovereign predestination in the cross is painted upon the background of the reality of man's total depravity, of man's totally, hopelessly lost estate by nature. On the other hand, there is in the cross the focal point of the whole of the truth of salvation by grace as far as the irresistible calling and the preservation and the glorification of the saints are concerned, -- from this point of view, that it is in the cross and the atonement of our Lord Jesus Christ, that centrally and objectively all of the salvation of God's people, as it is actually realized in their hearts and lives, is concentrated. It is in the atonement that we have the guarantee, the absolutely certain guarantee, of the calling and of the preservation and of the final glorification of God's people. Salvation by sovereign grace is a closed system, — closed to any work and any boasting of man. It is from beginning to end the work of God alone. It is the realization of that which is set forth in Romans 8:29, 30 in the well-known words: "For whom he did foreknow, he also did predestinate to be conformed to the image of his Son, that he might be the firstborn among many brethren. Moreover whom he did predestinate, them he also called: and whom he called, them he also justified: and whom he justified, them he also glorified." What according to God's counsel was fixed and finished from all eternity, from before the foundation of the world, is realized and revealed in time.

After these introductory remarks, we turn to our subject proper: LIMITED ATONEMENT. I ask your attention for three aspects of this subject: 1) The Atonement; 2) The Limited Nature of the Atonement; 3) The Importance of Maintaining this Doctrine.

THE ATONEMENT

Let me say from the outset that I intend to follow the order and the instruction of the Second Head of Doctrine of the Canons of Dordrecht. It will be helpful to consult those articles.

In the first place, let me clarify the exact subject.

First of all, we should note that our subject concerns the suffering and death of our Lord Jesus Christ. This probably sounds like a truism. But it has this two-fold importance. In the first place, this means that in all that we say about the atonement we are dealing with an *historic fact*, something that is objectively real. We are not discussing something that remains to be accomplished or that remains to be completed, but something that has been accomplished nineteen hundred years ago. Whatever belongs to that atonement is finished! It belongs to the past! It is an accomplished fact! We must distinguish here between the work of Christ *for us*, as it was accomplished in the cross, and the work of Christ *in us*, as it is concerned with the realization,in the hearts and lives of God's people, of what was objectively finished at the cross. This realization and application of the benefits of salvation in the experience of God's people does not belong to our subject in this chapter. In the second place, this point is important because the question is not merely whether Christ suffered and died. But the question is: what is the meaning, the significance, of that death of Christ? That Christ died is a fact; and all Christendom recognizes that fact of Christ's death, regardless of what they say about the meaning of it. But there have been various answers given, in the course of church history, to the question what was accomplished by that suffering and death of our Lord Jesus Christ. Some say that it was merely an example. Others say, — this is the governmental theory, — that it was a demonstration of God's just government of the universe, designed to bring men to repentance and thus to save them. We say, on the basis of Scripture: the death of Christ was *atonement,* that is, payment for sin and purchase of righteousness and eternal life. Still more: we say that it was *vicarious* atonement. It was substitution. Christ atoned not for Himself, but as a substitute for others (whoever those others may be). Christ was a substitute for others. Still more: the Reformed faith maintains, on the basis of Scripture, that the death of Christ was *limited* vicarious atonement. That is, Christ atoned as a substitute not for all and every man, but for His elect people alone.

In the second place, let me clarify the terms.

Neither of these terms, *limited* or *atonement,* is found in our confessions. Nor will you find these terms in Scripture. The term *atonement* occurs sometimes in our King James Version where it could better be translated either by "reconciliation" or by "propitiation, covering." The terms *limited* and *atonement* are simply dogmatic terms which have grown up in the church's vocabulary and which are used to describe briefly a thoroughly Scriptural and confessional concept. The term *atonement* covers such confessional terms as *redemption, redeem, purchase, satisfy, propitiatory sacrifice,* etc. And it covers such Scriptural terms as *reconciliation, propitiation, ransom, purchase,* etc. It simply looks at all these various Scriptural and confessional terms from a very basic point of view, a point of view which as far as the term is concerned is closely related to the idea of reconciliation. Atonement is really in its root idea *at-one-ment.* It refers to the fact that through the death of Christ God wrought reconciliation.

Also the term *limited* is used dogmatically to describe briefly a thoroughly Scriptural and confessional truth. The term has been criticized because the term seems to imply a defect, a shortage, a limitation in the death of Christ. Substitutes have been suggested which perhaps are better: substitutes like *definite* or *particular.* From a practical point of view this does not mean much. For our purposes the term is very clear. It means, — and it means this to everyone who hears the term, — it means this, that Christ died and atoned *for the elect, and for them only.*

In the third place, let me clarify the subject historically.

The doctrine of limited atonement is the Reformed doctrine

concerning the death of Christ and the redemption of men thereby (as Canons II puts it in its title) as it was officially set forth over against the Arminian heresy of general, or universal, atonement. The Arminians' second article, the Second Article of the Remonstrance, teaches this:

> That, agreeably thereto (that is, in harmony with the Arminian doctrine of election set forth in their first article, HCH), Jesus Christ, the Saviour of the world, died for all men and for every man, so that he has obtained for them all, by his death on the cross, reconciliation and the forgiveness of sins; yet that no one actually enjoys this forgiveness of sins except the believer, according to the word of the Gospel of John 3:16: "God so loved the world that he gave his only begotten Son, that whosoever believeth in him should not perish, but have everlasting life." And in the First Epistle of John, 2:2: "And he is the propitiation for our sins; and not for ours only, but also for the sins of the whole world."

Hence, the Arminians teach: 1) That the atonement of Christ is for every individual man, so that Christ obtained reconciliation and forgiveness of sins for all men. 2) Yet this atonement is effectual only in the believers. Though Christ obtained reconciliation and forgiveness for all, not all enjoy this reconciliation and forgiveness, but only the believers. The Arminians, therefore, teach a general atonement of which the benefit and the effect is dependent upon faith. They teach a universal atonement, but not a universal salvation. And they really deny the whole idea of the atonement, as we shall see. It is also very significant to notice the texts which they quote. By their quotation of these texts they give expression to the common Arminian error of making the Scriptural term "world" equivalent to every individual man.

Over against this Arminian doctrine stands the Reformed doctrine in Canons II.

If you remember this, it really makes the whole issue of the atonement as it is currently being debated a very simple one. It is simply literally Arminian to teach that Christ died for all men. That is the literal teaching of the Arminians. And that is the literal teaching that is explicitly opposed by the positive truth in Canons II, the first part, and rejected outright in Canons II, the second part, or the Rejection of Errors. It is important that we keep our bearings in this regard and that we do not begin to imagine that it is possible at all to impose that Arminian idea on our Reformed confessions. This attempt has been made. It has been attempted to appeal to the confessions, and especially to the Canons, for support of the doctrine of universal atonement. Now

49

that is simply flying in the face of the confessions. Canons II would never have been written if it had not been for the rise of the Arminian doctrine of universal atonement. It would not have been necessary. It is utterly fallacious, therefore, to try to maintain the doctrine of universal atonement in the name of the Reformed faith!

The contents of the Canons, Second Head, bear out what I have just said about the historical background and about the fundamental position of the Reformed faith over against the Arminian heresy.

Let us note the specific elements of the atonement as set forth by our confessions.

In the first place, I call your attention to the key element of *satisfaction.* This is a key term in all our confessions. That is especially the case with the Canons. But this term is emphasized repeatedly in our Heidelberg Catechism too. The Canons, however, start out with this idea of *satisfaction.* In the last part of Article 1 they already mention it: "....which we cannot escape, unless satisfaction be made to the justice of God."

Atonement, in this connection, is a matter of strictest justice. There is no grace, there is no mercy, there is no blessing, except in the way of God's righteousness. God blesses the righteous, and He curses and punishes the wicked temporally and eternally. That is the first principle in this idea of satisfaction. That is Article 1:

> God is not only supremely merciful, but also supremely just. And his justice requires (as he hath revealed himself in his Word), that our sins committed against his infinite majesty should be punished, not only with temporal, but with eternal punishment, both in body and soul; which we cannot escape, unless satisfaction be made to the justice of God.

Sin, therefore, in relation to the justice of God, is *guilt.* It is *debt.* It is liability to punishment. And that punishment, according to God's justice, cannot be escaped, and man cannot be restored to God's favor, unless satisfaction is made not to the devil, but to God's justice. That satisfaction, very simply, means "to do enough, to make payment of a certain debt or obligation, according to the demand of justice." If, among men, such satisfaction is made, let us say, of a debt of $1000, then as soon as that satisfaction is made, that debt is gone. It has been removed. It is no more. That is satisfaction, and that is the effect of satisfaction. Thus, if satisfaction of the debt of sin is made for any man, then that man's debt of sin and guilt is gone! It is no more! From the moment that satisfaction has been made, that debt is forever removed. It is forever removed before the bar of God's justice, mind you! That means that God Himself for the sake of His own justice and righteousness cannot hold that debt against the man for whose debt satisfaction has been made. We are not yet up to the question for whom such satisfaction has been made: we will face that question later. But whoever the man may be for whom satisfaction has been made, his debt is gone before God! If that satisfaction embraces all men, then the debt of all men is removed. But whoever are included in that satisfaction, their debt is forever gone! Such is the idea of satisfaction. This key element of the atonement cannot be emphasized too strongly. It is safe to say that the whole Scriptural and confessional concept of the atonement stands or falls with this fundamental element.

In this connection, in the third place, we must remember that we ourselves cannot make this satisfaction. I need not go into detail on this score. That is simply the implication of the hopelessly lost state of the sinner as he is by nature. It is the implication of the doctrine of total depravity. We cannot make that satisfaction. On the contrary, we can only increase our debt. Such satisfaction can be made only by the free, loving, obedient bearing of the punishment of sin, bearing of death, bearing of all the agonies of everlasting hell, to the very end. When that burden of the wrath of God has been borne, when all the vials of God's wrath have been poured out over a man, and he has borne them freely, out of love, for the sake of the love of God and the righteousness of God, — then satisfaction has been made. And when atonement is made, that is what is accomplished. To make such atonement-by-way-of-satisfaction for men who could not make that satisfaction by themselves God sent His only begotten Son in the likeness of sinful flesh.

Such is satisfaction.

That is the teaching of our Canons. In the first few articles of the Second Head of Doctrine that idea of satisfaction occurs again and again. Moreover, anyone who is familiar with the Heidelberg Catechism will recall how much emphasis the Catechism places upon this idea of satisfaction. The Confession of Faith likewise stresses this idea (Articles 20 and 21).

This teaching of our confessions is the teaching of Scripture too. The term *satisfaction* itself is not a Scriptural term. But it is the key idea in all the Scriptural terms that set forth the meaning of the death of Christ. That is true of a term like *propitiation,* as in Romans 3:25: "Whom God hath set forth to

51

be a propitiation through faith in his blood, to declare his right-eousness for the remission of sins that are past...." The funda-mental idea in that propitiation is this satisfaction. The same is true of a Scriptural term like *ransom*. Satisfaction is the basic idea of ransom. When the Scriptures say in Matthew 20:28 that the "Son of man came not to be ministered unto, but to minister, and to give his life a ransom for many," the idea is that He makes satisfaction. He satisfies the just demand of the One Who sets that ransom-price. The same is true of *reconciliation.* "God was in Christ, reconciling the world unto himself, not imputing their trespasses unto them." II Cor. 5:19. How is that possible? How is it possible that God can reconcile the world unto Himself and not reckon their trespasses unto them? How is it possible in the light of God's righteousness? Only on this basis, that that demand of God's righteousness and justice is totally met. Satisfaction! And so all the other Scrip-tural terms referring to the atonement have this same idea of satisfaction at their core.

The second main element in the atonement is that of *substitu-tion.* The necessity of that substitution lies in the fact that we are unable to make satisfaction of ourselves. It lies in our total depravity. That is the historical reason for the necessity of the atonement. We are hopelessly lost! We can never deliver our-selves! Therefore a proper substitute was necessary. This idea is set forth very plainly in Article 2 of Canons II:

> Since therefore we are unable to make that satisfaction in our own persons, or to deliver ourselves from the wrath of God, he hath been pleased in his infinite mercy to give his only begotten Son, for our surety, who was made sin, and became a curse for us and in our stead, that he might make satisfaction to divine justice on our behalf.

This is the doctrine of *vicarious, or substitutionary, atone-ment.* You cannot state it any more plainly than the Canons state it. You cannot improve on that language. It is very plain. Our Lord Jesus Christ stood in the stead, in the place, of those for whom He died. Before the bar of God's justice He represented men. He was their substitute in a legal sense.

Notice again that this is a very exact relationship. Put these two ideas, that of satisfaction and that of substitution, together now. What is the result? That result is very exact. If one man satisfies for the debt of one thousand other men, — let us say, at the Old Kent Bank he pays off the mortgages for one thousand men, — then that relationship is such that the debt of those one thousand is paid, and not the debt of every mortgage-holder at

Old Kent Bank. That's the exactitude here. It is the same way with the cross, with Christ's atonement. Whoever are in Christ, whoever are represented by Him on the cross, in whosesoever place He stood before the bar of God's justice and satisfied, — their debt is paid. If all men were in Him, then the debt of all men is forever gone. Whoever are represented by Him, their debt is absolutely gone. God cannot and does not hold that debt against them any more in His judgment.

Such is the idea of *substitutionary* atonement.

Also this is not merely the doctrine of our confessions, but it is the teaching of Scripture itself. Scripture teaches this idea of substitution in more than one way. But there are especially two terms in the New Testament which express this idea of substitution. These terms are usually translated by the word "for" in our English Bible. One of these terms means literally "in the stead of." You find this term in Matthew 20:28: "Even as the Son of man came not to be ministered unto, but to minister and to give his life a ransom for (instead of, in the place of) many." The other term has fundamentally the same meaning. It is the expression "in behalf of, for the sake of." But that idea, "in behalf of," is possible only because Christ makes satisfaction *instead of, in the place of,* those for whom He dies. Notice how beautifully that is stated in the last part of Canons II, 2: "....who was made sin, and became a curse *for us and in our stead,* that he might make satisfaction to divine justice *on our behalf."* The second term you find, for example, in II Corinthians 5:21: "For he hath made him to be sin for (in behalf of) us, who knew no sin; that we might be made the righteousness of God in him." These are only two examples of many passages of Scripture in which this idea of substitution occurs.

The third element of the atonement is that of its *infinite value.* Let me warn from the outset that this infinite value must not be conceived of in terms of finite numbers. It is not a question of quantity, but of quality, of intrinsic worth.

That truth of the infinite value of the atonement answers these questions: how could the death of one cover many sinners? How is it that when Christ atoned, He did not simply atone one for one, but one for many? Or again: how could sin, which is against the infinite majesty of God and which calls down infinite divine wrath and which requires everlasting punishment, — how could that sin be atoned for in a *moment* in the suffering and death of our Lord Jesus Christ? All the infinite wrath of God was concentrated finally in that moment when the cry was pressed out of Jesus' soul, "My God, my God, why hast thou forsaken me?"

And that infinite value answers the question: how could we be raised out of our totally lost estate, not simply back to the state of Adam in paradise, but so that we were provided with an everlasting righteousness, which we could never lose? How could we be provided with the right to eternal life?

The answer is: it was the Son of God, the eternal and infinite God Himself, in the likeness of sinful flesh, but as a real and perfectly righteous and holy man, Who brought that satisfaction.

That is the basic idea also in that sometimes-debated expression in Article 3 of Canons II: "...abundantly sufficient to expiate the sins of the whole world." That cannot mean, you know, that Christ intended to die for the whole world conceived of as all men. That would be the Arminian doctrine. That is just exactly what the fathers were fighting against in Canons II. It does not mean that at all. The article does not say either that Christ made satisfaction for the whole world. The idea is that in itself that death of Christ is so precious that in itself it is sufficient for the whole world. If God had wanted to save the entire world, head for head and soul for soul, He would not have needed another sacrifice. As one of the theologians of Dordrecht put it in his written opinion for the Synod of Dordrecht, the death of Christ was in itself sufficient for the whole world and for a thousand more worlds like it! The death of the Son of God is of infinite value: there is no end to its intrinsic worth!

Finally, there is the element of the *efficacy* of the atonement. The atonement is efficacious. Actually this is not a separate element of the atonement. The term efficacious simply emphasizes the reality, the actuality, the accomplished factuality of the preceding elements. This is spoken of in Article 8 of Canons II. Let me quote that article right here:

> For this was the sovereign counsel, and most gracious will and purpose of God the Father, that the quickening and saving efficacy of that most precious death of his Son should extend to all the elect, for bestowing upon them alone the gift of justifying faith, thereby to bring them infallibly to salvation: that is, it was the will of God, that Christ by the blood of the cross, whereby he confirmed the new covenant, should effectually redeem out of every people, tribe, nation, and language, all those, and those only, who were from eternity chosen to salvation, and given to him by the Father; that he should confer upon them faith, which together with all the other saving gifts of the Holy Spirit, he purchased for them by his death; should purge them from all sin, both original and actual, whether committed before or after believing; and having faithfully preserved them even to the end, should at last bring them free from every spot and blemish to the enjoyment of glory in his own presence forever.

The main subject in this article is not efficacious grace or efficacious calling; that is the subject in Canons III, IV, which teaches the doctrine of irresistible, or efficacious grace. But the main subject here is the efficacy, the power to accomplish something, that is in that death of Christ itself. Such efficacy is implied in the atonement. Really, as far as the meaning is concerned, when you include in the atonement the elements of satisfaction and substitution and infinite value, you do not have to say "efficacious" in addition. Those three elements spell efficacy. But because the Arminians also talked about atonement and about satisfaction and substitution and meant by their teaching something that was *not* efficacious, that did not really accomplish something, it became necessary for the Reformed fathers to say, "Yes, but the death of Christ is *efficacious*." It is with this expression much as it is with the expression "total depravity." Depravity is always total. There is no such thing as a half rotten man. But because of the fact that some have tried to speak of a partial depravity, it has become necessary for Reformed people to add that word "total." Thus it is with "efficacious atonement." You cannot really conceive of a non-efficacious atonement. That is a contradiction in terms. A non-efficacious atonement would be an atonement that did not atone. It did not accomplish anything. The atonement, — such is the idea of efficacious atonement, — *really atoned!* It really satisfied for all who were in Christ, for all for whom Christ substituted! Mark you well, efficacious atonement does not mean that Christ's death really atoned for all who get into Christ, — now, consciously, by faith. But Christ died and atoned for all who were in Him, — nineteen hundred years ago, when He died. It accomplished something for all of them. Their guilt is forever gone. Righteousness and eternal life can never be denied them. Their right to all the blessings of salvation was forever established there, at the cross.

Notice, in connection with this doctrine of efficacious atonement, how in Article 8 of Canons II our fathers emphasized the *crucial element* in the efficacious death of Christ (the efficacy, the power of the death of Christ). They emphasize it twice. It is this, that Christ purchased for His people *faith.* Faith! The atonement does not mean that Christ purchased righteousness and eternal life and all the other blessings of salvation, and that now He says in the gospel, "Here is salvation, but it is up to you to believe." It does not mean that. Christ purchased faith. He guaranteed by that purchase of faith that all for whom He died will also believe and will also lay hold personally and consciously on all the benefits of salvation that are in that death of Christ.

Hence, according to Article 8, the present, subjective application of the blessings of salvation (which was God's purpose, His sovereign purpose), whereby I and all God's people come into the actual, conscious possession of salvation, — that application proceeds from, is based upon, is guaranteed by the atonement. All those blessings were once and for all time actually purchased, merited, obtained on the cross; and they belong to Christ and to all who were in Christ at the cross. All the saints that had gone before, the saints of the old dispensation, — they were in Christ at the cross. All the elect who lived at the time of Christ's earthly sojourn, whether they were conscious children of God or whether they still had to be converted, — they were in Christ at the cross. And all the people of God who were still to be born at that time and who are still to be born today, — they were in Christ at the cross. He was in their place. He was their representative. And for them all He purchased, once for all, all the blessings of salvation! That is the teaching of Article 8. Notice: "This was the sovereign counsel (that's beautiful, you know: it proceeds from God, from His eternal decree, HCH), and most gracious will and purpose (in the original that is: "and intention") of God the Father, *that the quickening and saving efficacy of the most precious death of his Son* should extend to all the elect, for *bestowing upon them alone the gift of justifying faith,* thereby to bring them infallibly to salvation: that is, it was the will of God, that Christ by the blood of the cross (that's the atonement, HCH), whereby he confirmed the new covenant, *should effectually redeem* (that's what Christ did when He died, HCH) out of every people, tribe, nation, and language, all those, and those only who were from eternity chosen to salvation, and given to him by the Father; that he should confer upon them *faith, which together with all the other saving gifts of the Holy Spirit, he purchased for them by his death;* should purge them from all sin, both original and actual, whether committed before or after believing; and having faithfully preserved them even to the end, should at last bring them free from every spot and blemish to the enjoyment of glory in his own presence forever." (emphasis mine, HCH)

Such is the beautiful truth of efficacious atonement, set forth here by our fathers in its relation to the actual application and realization of salvation all the way to final glory!

THE LIMITED NATURE OF THE ATONEMENT

It is not surprising, therefore, that this article of the Canons at the same time teaches *limited atonement.* This is obviously what the article teaches: "....all those, and those only, who were from eternity chosen to salvation...."

That the atonement is limited is inseparable from the truth that the atonement is efficacious.

This question is very simple in the light of what we have already said about the atonement. If the atonement is *satisfaction* in the true, factual sense of the word, and if the atonement is *substitutionary* satisfaction in the real sense of that term, and if therefore the atonement is efficacious, so that those included in it have their debt removed and have eternal righteousness and life merited for them, so that, having been objectively redeemed, ransomed, reconciled, they will surely be saved and become the actual possessors of salvation, -- then, I say, the matter of limited atonement is very simple. Those included in the atonement are surely saved. But all men are not saved. Hence, not all men were included in the atonement.

Who were included in the atonement?

The answer is that Christ died only for the elect, that is, for those whom God has chosen from eternity and sovereignly and whom He gave to Christ. God elected an entire church and all the individual members of that church; and He gave that entire church, with all its individual members, to Christ. Christ is their representative-head. In the judgment of God He represents them, takes the place of them, and of them only, at the cross.

This is the truth of limited, (or call it, if you will, definite, particular) atonement. It is a very simple doctrine. There is atonement, and therefore removal of guilt and forgiveness of sins and righteousness and all the benefits of salvation and eternal life, for the elect only in the cross. For all the rest, for the reprobate, there is nothing positive, there is no benefit, in that cross. Christ did not die for them; He did not represent them and take their place.

Moreover, -- and this is a beautiful truth which we should never overlook, -- that definite atonement is *personal*. Christ did not die indefinitely. And Christ did not die merely for a number of men, so that He provided salvation indefinitely for a certain total number of men, whoever they might turn out to be. But Christ died for all the elect and for each of them personally. God chose them. He chose them individually. From eternity He called them by name. And all of the elect personally God gave to Christ. Christ knew them all, even as they had been given to Him by the Father from all eternity. And He laid down His life for them, for all of them, for each of them, and for them only. All the elect, and they only, were therefore very really in Christ at the cross nineteen hundred years ago.

57

Thus the cross is the revelation of God's sovereign love: "Herein is love, not that we loved God, but that He loved us, and sent his Son to be the propitiation for our sins." I John 4:10

Such is the doctrine of the confessions. It is very explicitly the doctrine of Canons II, 8. The same truth is already taught in connection with the doctrine of election in Canons I, 7. But this truth is also taught throughout our confessions. When you find the term "us" in the Heidelberg Catechism and the Confession of Faith in connection with the atoning death of our Lord Jesus Christ, do not forget that this "us" is from the objective viewpoint not all men, but the elect. In no other way can this expression be understood. And what occurs in the Catechism and the Confession of Faith in that subjective form is set forth in our Canons objectively as the elect exclusively.

There are many, many passages of Scripture which teach this truth, either directly or by clear implication in the context.

Let me concentrate for a moment on just one beautiful passage: John 10:14, 15. The correct rendering of this text is found in the American Revised Version: "I am the good shepherd; and I know mine own, and mine own know me, even as the Father knoweth me, and I know the Father; and I lay down my life for the sheep."

Who are the sheep that are mentioned in this passage as those for whom Christ lays down His life? They are those whom the Father gave to Christ, that is, the elect. This is the plain teaching of the context. In verse 29 you also read of these sheep; and there Jesus says, "My Father, *which gave them me,* is greater than all..." (italics mine, HCH) And this is enforced by way of contrast in verse 26, where Jesus says to the unbelieving Jews who opposed Him at that occasion: "But ye believe not, because ye are not of my sheep, as I said unto you." Notice that! Do not change that around as though it reads, "Ye are not of my sheep because ye believe not." That is not the text. The text is: "Ye believe not because ye are not of my sheep." They were reprobate.

This also makes it plain already that the concept "sheep" is exclusive. The argument has been raised that John 10:14, 15 does not teach that Jesus atoned *only* for His sheep. But that is a very poor argument. In the first place, as also the theologians of Dordrecht already pointed out in connection with this passage, the text would make no sense if it did not mean the sheep exclusively. Why should Jesus say that He lays down His life for the sheep, if after all He died equally for all men? And, in the second place, the context draws a sharp contrast between those who are His sheep and those who are not His sheep. And that contrast has its origin in God's predestinating purpose!

But notice that in this passage there is not merely a cold doctrine of election. The warm, throbbing, vibrant knowledge of divine love from eternity is involved here. "I know mine own...." Christ knew the whole church and every member of that church when He laid down His life! That is because those sheep are those whom the Father gave Him. He knew them all! Adam was in Him. Abel was in Him. Noah was in Him. Abraham and Isaac and Jacob and all God's people of the old dispensation, -- they were in Him at the cross. He knew them. He knew them individually. He knew them in love. All His people of that time, His elect people, had been given Him, given Him individually, from eternity. He knew them! The apostle Paul was in Him. He had not been converted yet. But he was in Christ at the cross because God gave him to Christ from eternity. That is why later the apostle Paul can speak of the personal aspect of that definite atonement in the well-known words of Galatians 2:20: "I am crucified with Christ: nevertheless I live; yet not I, but Christ liveth in me: and the life which I now live in the flesh I live by the faith of the Son of God, who loved me, and gave himself for me." He is speaking here of something that took place at the cross in the year 33 A.D. Then Christ loved him and gave Himself for him! Even though the apostle Paul did not know Him yet, Christ loved him and gave Himself for him. The same is true of us as God's people today. That is why we can say in a personal confession of faith, "Christ died for *me*." That is based on an objective fact! That does not become true merely when I believe in Christ. It was so, -- from eternity, according to God's counsel! And it has been so historically ever since Christ's death at the cross. And because of that objective reality, you and I, when we come to a conscious faith - union with Christ, can also confess, "Christ died for *me!*"

That, briefly, is the truth of limited, that is, definite and personal atonement.

There are, of course, many other passages of Scripture which plainly teach this same truth. In fact, this is the current teaching of Scripture. In this connection, let me enumerate a few passages which very clearly teach that Christ's atonement was definite, that is, for the elect only. Isaiah 53:10 speaks of a definite "seed" which Christ shall see when His soul shall be made an offering for sin. In John 17 we find Christ's high-priestly prayer, offered immediately before He laid down His life and brought the perfect sacrifice for sin. The whole tenor of this prayer is definite. As the High Priest, our Lord Jesus Christ prays only for His own; as it were, laying down His life and going the way of the cross, He utters this prayer: "I have manifested thy name unto the men which thou gavest me out of the world: thine they were, and thou gavest them me....I pray for them; I pray not for the world, but for them which thou hast given me; for they are thine. And all mine are thine....And for their sakes I sanctify myself, that they also might be sanctified through the truth. Neither pray I for these alone, but for them also which shall believe on me through their word....Father, I will that they also, whom thou hast given me, be with me where I am; that they may behold my glory, which thou hast given me: for thou lovedst me before the foundation of the world." John 17:6, 9, 10, 19, 20, 24. In Acts 20:28 it is the *church of God* "which he hath purchased with his own blood." In Romans 8:32, when we read that God "spared not his own Son, but delivered him up for us all," that "us all" is very plainly the elect, according to the context. For in the immediately following verses we read this: "Who shall lay any thing to the charge of God's elect? It is God that justifieth. Who is he that condemneth? It is Christ that died, yea rather, that is risen again, who is even at the right hand of God, who also maketh intercession for us." And, finally, in Ephesians 1:7 we read this: "In whom we have redemption through his blood, the forgiveness of sins, according to the riches of his grace." And what is the context of these words? It is a context which speaks most plainly of God's predestinating purpose as the source of all the blessings of salvation, including this "redemption through his blood." Eph. 1:3-12.

One more point must be made in this connection. When Scripture speaks of the "world" and of "all men" in connection with the atoning death of our Lord Jesus Christ, it does not and it cannot possibly teach something contrary to the plain Scriptural teaching of definite atonement. To study all of the passages in which these terms occur would take us far afield. But there are two observations which I wish to make. In the first place, if these passages which speak of the "world" and of "all men" are explained as meaning every individual man, and if then the atonement is ascribed its full meaning of actual satisfaction for sin and actual substitution, then they prove too much. For then they necessarily lead to full-fledged universalism, that is, the doctrine that all men are saved. And if the latter consequence is not accepted, then one must needs accept the consequence of the denial of God's justice: for if Christ actually satisfied for the sins of all men, and if all men are not saved, then God does not deal justly. And let me add: neither consequence is acceptable in the light of Scripture. In the second place, the point must be made in the light of the truth of the unity of Scripture, that all such passages which speak of the "world" and of "all men" must needs be interpreted in harmony with the current teaching of Scripture that Christ atoned for the elect only. If this is not done, then the consequence that Scripture contradicts itself must be accepted; and this, of course, is an unacceptable consequence.

Yet the attempt has always been made, and is made today, to find something and to say something positive about salvation and about the love and favor of God with respect to those who were not in Christ at the cross, with respect to the reprobate. This usually does not happen, — at least, not in Reformed circles, — as long as you are talking only in the area of Canons II, that is, as long as the doctrine of the atonement as such is under discussion. This arises rather in the preaching. It arises in the practical area of the preaching of the gospel. There is a striving to say something positive, to present something positively good in that atonement of Christ in the preaching of the gospel *to all men.* This is the way the entire matter arose in Professor H. Dekker's writings. It arose out of the question concerning mission work, the question concerning what must be said in the preaching of the gospel on the mission field. In so far, from a Christian Reformed point of view, Prof. Dekker was consistent: he saw that if you wanted to be general in the preaching, you had to go back a step and be general as far as the death of Christ was concerned also. That is consistent; but it is consistently wrong! But there is the same striving on the part of others in various ways. To be sure, you expect that from all kinds of Arminian preachers. They believe in a general atonement; and they preach accordingly. But there is the same striving in the Reformed community. Some try to accomplish this goal of being general in the preaching by simply leaving the matter of Christ's death indefinite and vague in their preaching. They simply say: "Christ died for sinners." That is true, of course. But if that is all that is said, it is only a half-truth. And a half-truth is subterfuge! Others, -- and that seems to be the striving of the committee that studied the issues of the Dekker Case, — others try to speak of "non-saving benefits of the death of Christ." And although they also claim to maintain definite atonement, they nevertheless claim that those non-saving benefits somehow come from the death of Christ Who died only for the elect. How that is possible I don't know. If Christ died for the elect only, then there are no possible benefits in that death of Christ for anyone else but those for whom He died. That is plain! Others speak, sometimes without even defining it very carefully at all, of a universal gospel offer. Others say, — and I read this in the column about the Canons in *The Banner* of February 24, 1967, — that we must say in the preaching that Christ desires the salvation of all men, and that God desires not the death of any but the salvation of all.

You understand, that is where the difficulty has arisen. It has arisen not in this doctrine of limited atonement as such. But when that atonement is projected into the preaching, then it suddenly becomes general in one way or another. And that is all rooted in the First Point of 1924 and its general, well-meant offer of the gospel as an evidence of so-called common grace. Everyone has recognized this, as is very plain from the fact that no one thus far has written or said anything about the issues of the Dekker Case without bringing in 1924. It is this that has led Prof. Dekker and others, — I say again: consistently, from their point of view, — to this idea of general atonement. But also those who have criticized Prof. Dekker's position have nevertheless not been willing to embrace wholeheartedly the doctrine of limited atonement and to follow it through consistently, but have insisted on somehow maintaining a universal and general element in the contents of the preaching.

If you look at this attempt from the basis of the Reformed doctrine of limited atonement, it is an impossible attempt. The gospel that must be preached is the gospel of the cross, the gospel of Christ crucified. Our Canons say that, and Scripture says that. The apostle Paul says, "We preach Christ crucified." He says, "I was determined to know nothing else among you but Jesus Christ, and him crucified." That means, in the light of all that we have said, that Christ crucified is Christ crucified for the elect. However you describe those elect in the preaching, whether you describe them historically as believers, as penitent, as hungry and thirsty, etc., Christ crucified is Christ crucified for the elect! I do not say the truth, I do not present Christ crucified, therefore, if I merely say, "Christ died for sinners." And I certainly do not present the gospel of Christ crucified when I say, "Christ died for all men." And in so far as that cross is the revelation of God's desire, God's purpose, God's will, I do not say the truth of the gospel of Christ crucified when I say, "God desires the salvation of all men." He does not. He reveals very plainly in the cross that He purposed and desired and intended and counselled the salvation of the elect, and of them only.

Often this disjunction between Christ's death only for the elect and God's purported desire for the salvation of all men is presented as a mystery. But that is no mystery. If you say that

Christ died for the elect, and for them only, and that God desires the salvation of all men, that is no mystery, but a flat contradiction. That is impossible. It is impossible because there is nothing positive, no benefit, no salvation, no love, no so-called non-saving benefit, — nothing positive whatsoever, — in that cross for anyone but the elect. And that cross is the revelation of God's purpose of salvation. To say otherwise, to make the scope of salvation wider in the preaching than it is in the cross is an implicit denial of particular atonement. The gospel is God's good news concerning the promise, to make known unto the heirs of the promise, that is, the elect, their salvation.

That is the positive side of the cross and of the atonement.

That is leaving out of the picture yet the fact that there was judgment at the cross, — judgment as well as salvation. Wrath as well as favor were revealed in the cross and are proclaimed in the gospel of Christ crucified. Indeed, there is nothing positive for the reprobate in the cross. But that does not mean that the cross is of no significance for them. The wrath of God is revealed in the cross as well as the love of God.

That is why our Lord Jesus Christ could say in John 12:31, for example, with a view to the death that He would die: "Now is the judgment of this world: now shall the prince of this world be cast out." And not only does our Lord Jesus Christ repeatedly make plain that He has come into the world for judgment (cf. passages like John 9:39, Matthew 21:21-43, etc.), but we must remember that the first coming of our Lord belongs to "the great day of the Lord" of which the prophets speak so often and in connection with which they also always speak of God's judgment. In that same connection we may note that John the Baptist, the forerunner, preaches Christ under the aspect of judgment: the axe is laid to the root of the trees! And the apostle Paul refers to this same element of the judgment of the cross in Colossians 2;14, 15: "Blotting out the handwriting of ordinances that was against us, which was contrary to us, and took it out of the way, nailing it to his cross; And having spoiled principalities and powers, he made a shew of them openly, triumphing over them in it."

Let me briefly sketch this idea.

There was a trial at the cross. There was not merely a trial of Jesus by men. But there was a trial of the world by God. The world outside of Christ, the world of sinful men, the world in their state of sin and guilt, the world of men as they are in the present creation with all their means of subsistence and development, all their means of "culture," — that world was on trial. The whole world of men as they are in Adam, by nature, together with the prince of this world, the devil, and all the fallen angels, the principalities and powers, the whole world, our world (apart from Christ) as it is in alliance with and under the moral dominion of the prince of darkness — that whole world was on trial before God, the Judge. God summoned them there. He controlled the events surrounding the suffering and death of Christ. Christ went to the cross, remember, according to the determinate counsel and foreknowledge of God, though by wicked hands.

That world was well represented. It was represented in Judas, the apostle. It was represented religiously in the Sanhedrin. The world of men at large, of society, was represented in the multitude. The political world-power, the Graeco-Roman world of wisdom and justice, was represented. The world in all its aspects was put on trial.

That trial consisted in this. They were openly exposed. They were stripped naked, as the apostle Paul says in Colossians 2:15. They were cloaked in self-righteousness and wisdom and religion and jurisprudence. They were masked! And they could not go to hell with a mask on! They had to be exposed. God exposed them. He stripped them bare. He did that by standing before them in the person of our Lord Jesus Christ as a man, without power, and by confronting them with the question, "What will you do with God? What will you do with God if He stands before you as a mere man, a man without a sword, a man without an army, a man without any defense except the defense of righteousness, a man who will not fight back against you?"

They were compelled to give answer to that question. They tried to avoid it. Pilate, for example, especially tried in various ways to avoid answering that crucial question. But the Judge of heaven and earth insisted: "Give an answer!"

And they answered: "We will kill Him! We will nail Him to the cross!"

It was at the cross that the verdict of the Judge of heaven and earth was rendered and executed. When the trial was finished, God poured out the vials of His wrath. The world was proven worthy of the wrath of God; and the execution followed at Golgotha, — in the cross, in the darkness, in that fearful revelation of God-forsakenness! And Christ was in the center of it all! Christ as representing His own, Christ representing the whole world of God's election, was in the center of that fearful outpouring of judgment and wrath. And all the vials of God's wrath were concentrated in one hour, the hour of judgment! And God was there, in behalf of the world of His election, bearing His own wrath in our flesh!

The result?

The world in itself, the world outside of Christ, was condemned! That is revealed at the cross too. The veil is rent: God leaves the temple, and Israel is forsaken. The earth quakes, and the rocks split, signifying that this world must pass away. That is even evident in the two thieves at the cross: only one of them was saved, covered by that cross of Christ.

And yet, in Christ the world, that is, the world of God's love and God's election, is justified.

The judgment is past! The last day, the day of the revelation of God's righteous judgment shall finally reveal the condemnation of the world in itself and the justification of the world in Christ.

To that end the church must preach the gospel, the gospel of absolutely sovereign grace, revealed in Christ crucified. To that end the church must preach the gospel of Christ crucified: Christ crucified, to the Jews a stumbling block, and to the Greeks foolishness (that is, to the natural man, whether Jew or Greek, a power of God unto condemnation); but to them that are called, both Jews and Greeks, Christ the power of God and the wisdom of God.

It is this negative aspect of the cross and this negative aspect of the gospel that is completely forgotten and denied nowadays for the most part. For the most part, the church no longer is willing to be obedient to its calling to preach the gospel negatively as well as positively. It is no longer willing to preach Christ crucified as the power of God, Who is really God. The church would much rather preach a Christ and a God Whose salvation are, after all, dependent upon the will and the choice of the fallen sinner.

THE IMPORTANCE OF MAINTAINING THIS TRUTH

This precious truth must be maintained. It must be maintained as far as the atonement is concerned, and it must be maintained as far as the negative aspect of the cross and of the gospel is concerned.

That is important for us, first of all, as individual believers.

For remember: a Christ for all is really a Christ for none! You must choose between a general atonement which actually is not atonement or vicarious and limited atonement which is real and efficacious. After all, if Christ actually atoned vicariously for all men, then all men must be saved. But even the Arminian, who holds to general atonement, must face the fact that all men are not saved. Hence, the Arminian presentation of the atonement comes down to this: Christ died for all men, but all men are not justified and saved. What follows from this? This: Christ's atonement was ineffectual. I cannot be sure that He atoned for any man, including myself. Thus the believer is deprived of the solid basis of assurance that there is in the atoning death of the cross.

In the second place, this is important for the church and its gospel-proclamation. I am well aware that this is a foreign note in our day. It sounds so sweet and so humane to proclaim a Christ for all and a love of God for all. And it has become very popular. It is claimed that it is impossible to preach and to do mission work without a general gospel and a general salvation. Basically, however, the trouble is that men do not want to put their confidence in a cross that is the power of God! Nor do they want to trust that God will surely use the general proclamation of a particular promise to gather and save His elect church.

But remember that the gospel cannot possibly be wider in scope than the objective satisfaction and justification of the cross of our Lord Jesus Christ. If you hold to a general, well-meaning offer, you must and you will, if you are consistent, ultimately embrace the doctrine of universal atonement also.

The proof, — I call you to witness, — is already here!

Hence, we must stand one hundred per cent in the truth of our Reformed confessions, both with respect to the atonement and the preaching. And if we have already departed from that, we must return and forsake what is false.

May God lay this upon your heart and mine.

Chapter IV

Irresistible Grace

Irresistible Grace

Gise J. Van Baren

I have in my possession several exhibits. First, I have a check, rather widely distributed, and sent out evidently in order to encourage others to be saved. It is dated: "Anytime, anywhere." It is written out on the "Bank of the Riches of Jesus — Resources Unlimited." It is written out to be paid to the order of the bearer on demand "his need according to the riches in glory by Christ Jesus." Among other things, the explanation on the back states this: "Will you take Him today as your Savior? Friend, don't turn Him away. He's waiting to receive you. He is longing to bless and to save you. He wants to give you eternal life. And if you accept Him, he will fill your soul with a joy such as you have never known in all your life and make you a child of God, an heir of God, and a joint-heir with Jesus Christ." Now I ask you, what kind of God is this Who must await the endorsement of the sinner before He can confer upon him this salvation?

Here is a second exhibit. I have a ballot, an opportunity to vote for your salvation. This "ballot" has also been widely distributed to promote "acceptances" of Christ. There are three who vote on this ballot, and each can vote in one of two ways. First, God votes -- and He votes "yes" for your salvation. Secondly, the devil votes — and he votes "no." Then there is your vote — and two possibilities are presented: "yes" or "no." Your vote becomes the deciding vote. The idea is that man's final salvation is determined by himself. And I ask again, what kind of God is this Who, though He votes, must await your vote before your salvation is finally determined?

Another exhibit I have from *The World Aflame* by Billy Graham. He writes this, "There is also volitional resolution. The will is necessarily involved in conversion. People can pass through mental conflicts and emotional crises without being converted. Not until they exercise the prerogative of a free moral agent and will to be converted are they actually converted. This act of will is an act of acceptance and commitment. They willingly accept God's mercy and receive God's Son and then

69

commit themselves to do God's will. In every true conversion the will of man comes into line with the will of God. Almost the last word of the Bible is this invitation: 'And whosoever will, let him take of the water of life freely' (Rev. 22:17). It is up to you. You must will to be saved. It is God's will, but it must become your will, too." (Pg. 134, pocket-book edition). I ask you again, what kind of God is this Who wills your salvation, but now is eagerly awaiting your will to be made conformable to His?

These examples set before us the Arminianism of our day which would deny those important Scriptural truths concerning our salvation. We do indeed today have the threat of another evil: modernism. This denies the cross of Christ itself and denies the glory which is promised us for Jesus' sake. Yet it is implied far too often that the alternative to modernism is Arminianism. It is suggested, even among those within Reformed circles, that because these do speak of the cross of our Lord Jesus Christ, we should cooperate with them and encourage them. You understand, do you not, that these exhibits which I have presented above do mention the cross of our Lord Jesus Christ -- nevertheless these deny the *power* of God and the *power* of the cross of His Son. No, Arminianism does not deny *all* of God's power, nor *all* of the power of the cross, but it denies *much* of it. Arminianism would place such power in your hands whereby you finally must determine your own salvation. Is it really a matter worthy of debate -- this subject of Arminianism? Two things one must remember. In the first place, our subject is not simply that which is interesting, but basically unimportant; rather we deal with God as He has been pleased to reveal Himself in His infallible Word. Neither you nor I may just say anything we please about God. We must, on the contrary, maintain Him and confess His Name as He has revealed Himself in His Word. And we must confess His work as He has set it forth in this Word -- which work we have experienced within our own hearts. We are treating the subject of the salvation of God's church, and it makes a world of difference how we believe this salvation takes place.

In this chapter, your attention is called to that fourth point of the five points of Calvinism: Irresistible Grace. Notice, first of all, what this grace of God is; secondly, notice its irresistibility; finally, notice its comfort.

QUESTIONS CONCERNING OUR SALVATION

Questions do arise in the study of the truths related to our salvation. Questions there are with respect to the three points of Calvinism which have already been presented in preceding chapters. The question arises when one speaks of the wonderful truths of unconditional election and limited atonement, "How am I ever to be a partaker of that? Am I, who am no better nor different than anyone else, a beneficiary of that limited atonement of Christ? How does this come to be? Is it because God nevertheless has seen in me something that He has not seen in others? Is it because in me there is found some willingness and desire to follow after Him, that is not found in others?" But that can not be; for with all those born of Adam, I am totally depraved.

Another question arises: "If it is true, and I believe it is, that I am a beneficiary of that atonement of the cross, how is this *applied* to me? How do I enjoy those benefits of that salvation merited for me by my Lord Jesus Christ? Do I receive His benefits because I am *willing* to come to Him? Do I receive these benefits because I am ready to endorse the check He offers to me?" But that also can not be.

SAVED BY GRACE ALONE

The answer of all Scripture is: I am partaker of Christ's atonement (even as God has eternally chosen me before the foundation of the earth) by the free, sovereign, unmerited, grace of God. Read it in Ephesians 2:8, "For by grace are ye saved through faith, and that not of yourselves: it is the gift of God." We are "saved by grace through faith" -- and that is the only possible way. "FOR ye are saved by grace," says that Word of God. That is the basis and foundation of the salvation of God's church. (By grace, and by grace alone) He has chosen unto Himself a people from before the foundations of the earth in Christ. By grace alone He sends forth His Word and Spirit and calls forth that new life of regeneration, which the Spirit instills in our hearts, drawing His people from darkness into His marvelous light. By grace, and by grace alone, we are preserved daily until finally we are brought to eternal glory. Indeed: "by grace are ye saved through faith."

THE IDEA OF THE GRACE OF GOD

What is that grace which saves? I can not begin to present the many texts of Scripture that speak of grace. Nor is it possible in this short essay to treat in detail the various elements of the grace of God. Yet there are several truths which we ought to know of grace. Concerning the idea of grace, there are especially two elements which require emphasis. In the first place, the root idea of grace is beauty. One who is gracious is one who is lovely in appearance. Secondly, the term grace suggests favor which is shown to another. Oftentimes in Scripture the term grace is so used. We read of those which find grace or favor in the eyes of another.

71

Now grace, despite some who deny this, is an attribute of God. Grace is that attribute of God which emphasizes the fact of His infinitely glorious perfection. All righteousness, truth, holiness, and love are found without measure in the living God. These infinite perfections are His beauty or grace. The Psalmist David saw that in Psalm 27:4, "One thing have I desired of the Lord, that will I seek after; that I may dwell in the house of the Lord all the days of my life, to behold the beauty of the Lord, and to enquire in his temple." That "beauty" is the grace of God.

One must say more of this grace of God. The grace of God within Himself is the attribute in which He as the triune God *beholds* His own perfections, and finds favor in His own eyes with respect to Himself. The triune God, beholding Himself, rejoices eternally that He *is* the God of all perfections.

The same grace of God He has been pleased to reveal outside of Himself. This attribute of God is reflected towards and in His people for His own Name's sake. We read in Romans 5:15, "But not as the offense, so also is the free gift. For if through the offence of one many be dead, much more the grace of God, and the gift by grace, which is by one man, Jesus Christ, hath abounded unto many." God has been pleased to reveal His own perfections outside of Himself to that people whom He has eternally chosen by grace. This grace of God to His people is *unmerited* favor. Do we not usually use that term in this way? Scripture, and we, speak of the contrast between grace and works. Scripture declares in Romans 4:4, "Now to him that worketh is the reward not reckoned of grace, but of debt." Notice the contrast between works and grace in this passage? Grace is here the undeserved, unmerited favor which God is pleased to work in us for Jesus' sake. It is unmerited because we deserve nothing of that given. I am dead in sins. I deserve nothing. I can earn nothing. That which God bestows upon me is not earned by me, but is given solely by His free grace.

In the third place, this grace of God is grace that *works*. This favor of God that He reflects to and in His people is a beauty that is *power*. It fashions and forms His people according to God's own design. Remember what the apostle Paul said in I Corinthians 15:10? "But by the grace of God I am what I am...." What a brief statement — but what a wealth of meaning! Paul had persecuted the church in the past; he had pursued them even to Damascus; he had imprisoned them and participated in killing them. This same Paul was taken by that marvelous, completely unmerited grace of God, and was turned so that the persecutor now himself became the persecuted as a result of his union to

72

Christ. Now Paul was imprisoned and mocked and whipped. "By grace," he says, "I am what I am." The power of God's grace fashions His people. He forms them that they may show forth His praise. That is the grace of our God.

But what is the significance of such a grace? Do not forget, first of all, the power of this grace. It is not simply an influence, but the very power of God that accomplishes what He determined to do. Secondly, this power of grace is revealed only in and through His only begotten Son Jesus Christ. He has been pleased to show His favor in no other way than through Jesus. It is shown to no other people than to those who have been united to His Son. Finally, this too we must remember: there is only *one* grace of God. That grace which exists within God Himself is the grace which He reveals outside of Himself. And that grace outside of Himself is revealed only to His people and to none other.

GRACE WHICH IS IRRESISTIBLE

The grace of God is irresistible. You understand what the term "irresistible" suggests. Do not think that irresistible grace is some sort of blind force which simply drags the struggling, rebellious sinner into heaven against his will — as a policeman might drag a rebellious prisoner to jail. The grace of God is not such a power that compels to enter into heaven those who would not.

That God's grace is irresistible emphasizes the idea that not only does grace *bring* His people to glory, but it *prepares* them for this glory and works within them the desire to enter into glory. Grace is irresistible in the sense that by it the knee is bent which otherwise would not bend; the heart is softened that otherwise is hard as stone. Nor is there anything which can prevent the accomplishment of that purpose of God to save His people by His grace.

THE DENIAL OF IRRESISTIBLE GRACE

Not all confess the truth of the irresistible grace of God. One who believes that Christ died for *all* sinners, can not believe the truth of irresistible grace. There are those who maintain, as we do, that one is saved by grace alone. These maintain, as we do, that the sinner apart from grace can never be saved. These maintain, as we do, that only by the power of God's grace does the sinner bow the knee; only by grace does one come to Christ; only by grace is one preserved and guided in his way. "BUT," say these, "this grace of God is a grace administered to all, head for head, so that those who otherwise could not, now can accept

Christ and desire to be saved *if they will.*" This is the old heresy of Arminianism.

You recall James Arminius, a Dutchman. Under his instigation, many in the Reformed Church of the Netherlands departed from the old truths of Scripture. At that time, in 1610, those who opposed Calvinism drew up a document called *The Five Articles of the Remonstrance,* or, *The Five Arminian Articles.* Five articles these were that opposed the five truths which we are considering in this booklet. The fourth article of that document treats the subject of the resistibility of grace. It reads as follows:

> That this grace of God is the beginning, continuance, and accomplishment of all good, even to this extent, that the regenerate man himself, without prevenient or assisting, awakening, following and co-operative grace, can neither think, will, nor do good, nor withstand any temptations to evil; so that all good deeds or movements, that can be conceived, must be ascribed to the grace of God in Christ. But as respects the mode of the operation of this grace, it is not irresistible, inasmuch as it is written concerning many, that they have resisted the Holy Ghost. Acts 7, and elsewhere in many places.

Do you follow the argument? It is all of grace whereby one is saved. But all receive this grace. And one not saved, is unsaved because he resisted the grace given him. On the other hand, when one is saved, it is because he received that grace and accepted Christ. Thus salvation comes forth from that man who does not resist God's grace. But if a man rejects that grace, the Holy Spirit is utterly helpless with respect to him, says the Arminian.

James Arminius himself in his *Complete Works* (Vol. 1, pages 253-254) states it virtually the same way. Seeking to show the validity of his views, he writes:

> In this manner, I ascribe to grace THE COMMENCEMENT, THE CONTINUANCE AND THE CONSUMMATION OF ALL GOOD, and to such an extent do I carry its influence, that a man, though already regenerate, can neither conceive, will, nor do any good at all, nor resist any evil temptation, without this preventing and exciting, this following and co-operating grace. From this statement it will clearly appear, that I by no means do injustice to grace, by attributing, as it is reported of me, too much to man's free-will. For the whole controversy reduces itself to the solution of this question, "is the grace of God a certain irresistible force?" That is, the controversy does not relate to those actions or operations which may be ascribed to grace, (for I acknowledge and inculcate as many of these actions or operations as any man ever did,) but it relates solely to the mode of

74

operation, whether it be irresistible or not. With respect to which, I believe, according to the scriptures, that many persons resist the Holy Spirit and reject the grace that is offered.

It is this idea which the Reformed churches have ever opposed. We *must* oppose that — this idea that the sovereign glorious unmerited grace of God is resistible.

IRRESISTIBLE GRACE: A CALVINISTIC TRUTH

But we must have proof that grace is irresistible. In the first place, I would remind you that this truth of irresistible grace necessarily follows out of the preceeding points of Calvinism which have already been treated in previous chapters: total depravity, unconditional election, and limited atonement. One can not maintain total depravity, yet deny irresistible grace. Can you see that? If the sinner is totally depraved, dead in sin, unable to do any good, then he needs far more than mere *assistance*. Give a dead man a cane and try thus to assist him in walking! You know that such assistance would be of no avail. Rather, he must be made alive again or he will never walk. So it is with the totally depraved sinner. God does not give to every totally dead sinner some sort of cane (grace) and say, "Here is something to assist you; now serve me!" God does not do that. On the contrary, His grace must take the dead sinner and must make him alive again. Total depravity implies that an *irresistibly* powerful grace of God is the only hope for the dead sinner.

The same can be said of unconditional election: this truth implies necessarily an irresistible grace of God. God has chosen unto Himself a people from before the foundations of the earth. The execution of the decree of God can not rest now upon the fickle will of man, but rests upon the irresistible grace of God which will surely bring to realization His eternal purpose.

Limited atonement is also inseparably related to God's grace. In the atonement, we confess, Christ dies only for His people on the cross, redeeming them fully from their sins. Now, how does this work of Christ become ours? Does it rest upon your will whether or not you shall receive that atonement? And could God allow the death of His Son to come to naught in that some for whom He died would not be saved? God forbid! When His Son pays for the sins of His people, it is the power of God's grace whereby the life of Christ is given to His own and they are brought unto eternal life.

IRRESISTIBLE GRACE: A SCRIPTURAL TRUTH

But you want proof from Scripture. And Scriptural proof you shall have. What does God teach of this in His Word? The

Arminian would have us consider Acts 7. Acts 7, says he, teaches a resistible grace of God. Let us examine that passage. Verse 51 states: "Ye stiffnecked and uncircumcised in heart and ears, ye do always resist the Holy Ghost: as your fathers did, so do ye." Stephen addresses the Jews who were about to stone him. "Ye do always resist the Holy Ghost," he says. Does it not from this appear that God's grace is after all resistible? Other passages of Scripture apparently speak in this same vein. But remember: in Acts 7 Stephen is speaking to the Jews concerning the words of the prophets which came to the Jews in the past. In resisting the words of these prophets, the Jews had resisted the Holy Ghost. How did they do that? The Holy Ghost reveals God's Word to holy men: prophets and apostles. The Holy Ghost uses ministers of the Word to proclaim the Word of God throughout all ages: to the Jew of the Old Dispensation, and to every tribe and tongue and language in the New. And what do these who hate the Word do? They resist; they rebel; they show scorn. They take those whom the Holy Ghost uses to proclaim the Word, and kill them. Of all this Stephen is speaking. He is not telling them that the Spirit of God was given to all to lead all to repentance — but many resisted. Certainly not. But the Spirit is resisted when these resist the holy men whom the Spirit sends.

Now consider some other pertinent passages of Scripture. Read John 3:3 and 5 particularly, "Jesus answered and said unto him, Verily, verily, I say unto thee, Except a man be born again, he can not see the Kingdom of God.... Verily, verily, I say unto thee, Except a man be born of water and of the Spirit, he can not enter into the kingdom of God." What does this passage teach? There is presented, first, the picture of a birth — a new birth. What does that mean? In physical birth, does the one that is born exercise his own will in order to come forth? Is it according to his will that he is either conceived or brought forth? Impossible! One is born into this sinful world, and he must live here his allotted life span. Therefore Scripture uses the term "new birth." That phrase "born again" serves to emphasize what happens in the realm of the spiritual. God is not waiting to see if any will desire to be born again, but God forms a people unto Himself by giving unto them the life of our Lord Jesus Christ. He causes also that life to grow and develop. "Except ye be born of water and of the Spirit, ye can not enter into the kingdom of God." Ah, yes; it is this irresistible grace that brings to the birth the elect of God. Besides, the term "born again" can also be translated "born from above." Again, that same passage states: "Except a man be born again he can not SEE the kingdom of God." One who can not *see* this kingdom, can not even believe that it exists. That is the meaning of this passage which states that no man can *see* the kingdom of heaven except he is born again. Surely this emphasizes that there is not in the dead sinner a will which he can exercise in order to see. It is by the irresistible grace of God that one is born again. *Only* then can he see.

Turn now to Ephesians 2:10, "For we are his workmanship, created in Christ Jesus unto good works, which God hath before ordained that we should walk in them." Whose is this work of salvation? We are *His* workmanship. An artist forms his work as he will. The artist does not ask the clay which he forms, "In what form would you desire to be made?" But he fashions the clay according to his own will. So also we are God's workmanship. God Himself forms His people to be what they now are. The prophet states this too in Isaiah 43:21, "This people have I formed for myself; they shall show forth my praise." That is irresistible grace. This power of God does not wait for those poor miserable sinners to accept Christ — but it *forms* them to be His people. They therefore show forth His praise.

Now read John 6:37, "All that the Father giveth me shall come to me; and him that cometh to me I will in no wise cast out." Verse 44, "No man can come to me, except the Father which hath sent me draw him: and I will raise him up at the last day." Verse 65, "And he said, Therefore said I unto you, that no man can come to me, except it were given unto him of my Father." Notice: no man can come unto Christ *except it were given* unto him of the Father. All that the Father giveth *shall come.* How? These come because, "My Father," says Jesus, "shall *draw* him and I will raise him up again in the last day." That is the ir- resistible grace of God which takes the dead sinner and brings him to Christ.

Now recall that wonderful Lydia of Acts 16, "And a certain woman named Lydia, a seller of purple, of the city of Thyatira, which worshipped God, heard us: whose heart the Lord opened, that she attended unto the things which were spoken of Paul." Lydia's heart is opened by the Lord. This has an entirely diff- erent sound than that class of religious songs which is heard today proclaiming, "Open your heart and let Him come in." You have heard such. And the evangelist of this day declares, "Christ stands waiting at your heart's door; won't you let Him in before it is too late?" I quoted that from the "gospel check" too: "Open up your heart and let Him in." But Scripture never says that. It is true that in Revelation 3:20 Jesus is presented as knocking at the door. But this is not the door of anyone's heart. He knocks at the door of that corrupt church of Laodicea and He calls unto separation those who yet love the Word of God. But

Christ does not knock at any man's heart. The Lord opened Lydia's heart — then she listened and believed. That is the irresistible power of the grace of our God. He breaks open the closed heart; and the child of God believes.

We read in Acts 13:48, "...and as many as were ordained to eternal life believed." This too emphasizes the idea I suggested earlier: those whom God has chosen, He also will surely save. The ones He has ordained to eternal life, believe. What is the explanation for that? Is there a willingness within them? Oh, no. Only the irresistible grace of God accomplishes that which He has eternally determined to do.

IRRESISTIBLE GRACE: A CONFESSIONAL TRUTH

Our confessions teach the same thing. The Canons of Dort especially state this truth more beautifully than I ever could. I quote from the third and fourth head of doctrine, Article 10:

> But that others who are called by the gospel, obey the call, and are converted, is not to be ascribed to the proper exercise of free will, whereby one distinguishes himself above others, equally furnished with grace sufficient for faith and conversions, as the proud heresy of Pelagius maintains; but it must be wholly ascribed to God, who as he has chosen his own from eternity in Christ, so he confers upon them faith and repentance, rescues them from the power of darkness, and translates them into the kingdom of his own Son, that they may show forth the praises of him, who hath called them out of darkness into his marvelous light; and may glory not in themselves, but in the Lord according to the testimony of the apostles in various places.

That is the confession of all those truly Reformed. Article 11 of the same confession states:

> But when God accomplishes his good pleasure in the elect, or works in them true conversion, he not only causes the gospel to be externally preached to them, and powerfully illuminates their minds by his Holy Spirit, that they may rightly understand and discern the things of the Spirit of God; but by the efficacy of the same regenerating Spirit, pervades the inmost recesses of the man; he opens the closed, and softens the hardened heart, and circumcises that which was uncircumcised, infuses new qualities into the will, which though heretofore dead, he quickens; from being evil, disobedient, and refractory, he renders it good, obedient, and pliable; actuates and strengthens it, that like a good tree, it may bring forth the fruits of good actions.

The other articles are also pertinent. Read them. This is the confession of Reformed churches in which they express what they believe the Word of God plainly teaches.

Other confessions of the church teach this same truth. The Westminster Confession, Article 10 of Chapter 1 states:

> All those whom God hath predestinated unto life, and those only, he is pleased, in His appointed and accepted time, effectually to call, by His Word and Spirit, out of that state of sin and death, in which they are by nature, to grace and salvation by Jesus Christ; enlightening their minds, spiritually and savingly, to understand the things of God; taking away their heart of stone, and giving unto them an heart of flesh; renewing their wills, and by His almighty power determining them to that which is good, and effectually drawing them to Jesus Christ; yet so as they come most freely, being made willing by His grace.

Is the picture clear? Both the confession of Scripture and the confessions of the church based upon Scripture express that the grace of God is His irresistible power whereby He saves His people in Christ.

THE COMFORT OF THIS TRUTH

But does it mean anything to you? What does this irresistible grace of God mean to you? It must mean something. It is the basis of comfort for the Christian. Imagine once that we were to deny this irresistible grace of God. That would mean first of all, of course, that we would be denying what Scripture itself teaches concerning the power of God's grace. That is a serious thing in itself, to trifle with the revelation which God gave concerning Himself. But also, were His grace resistible, it would mean that all assurance would be gone concerning my salvation. I have a will which is no different from that of any other man. If God's grace were merely an influence which could be resisted, then I would be lost -- for I would never will my salvation. If I *can* resist, I *will* resist. If that grace of God were resistible, no Christian could endure in this evil age. I can stand only by a grace which not only saves me, but holds me daily to the end.

That is our comfort, and the comfort of our children: the irresistible grace of God not only draws me, but preserves and glorifies me for Jesus' sake. I am saved to the uttermost by the power of God's grace. The devil can never change that -- nor can evil men of this age. These will try, but they can never take us from the Father's hand. The old nature which loves the world and seeks the things of darkness can not oppose successfully that irresistible grace of God. For His grace comes and breaks me down. It softens my hard heart. It bows my stiff knee. It takes my arm which would by nature raise itself in rebellion against God, and causes it to beat upon my breast so that I cry out, "O God, be merciful to me the sinner." That is the irresistibility of the grace of our God. It makes me His child. It leads me in paths of righteousness. And it finally glorifies me according to His promise for His Name's sake through Jesus Christ our Lord.

Then we can sing with that poet of old who also must have experienced the wonder of that irresistible grace of God, for he cried out:

> Amazing grace, how sweet the sound!
> That saved a wretch like me.
> I once was lost, but now am found;
> Was blind, but now I see.
> 'Twas grace that taught my heart to fear,
> And grace my fears relieved;
> How precious did that grace appear
> The hour I first believed.

Chapter V

The Perseverance Of The Saints

The Perseverance Of The Saints

Gise J. Van Baren

We read in Rev. 21, "And I saw a new heaven and a new earth: for the first heaven and the first earth were passed away; and there was no more sea. And I, John, saw the holy city, new Jerusalem, coming down from God out of heaven, prepared as a bride adorned for her husband. And I heard a great voice out of heaven saying, 'Behold, the tabernacle of God is with men, and He will dwell with them, and they shall be His people, and God Himself shall be with them, and be their God. And God shall wipe away all tears from their eyes; and there shall be no more death, neither sorrow, nor crying, neither shall there be any more pain: for the former things are passed away.' And He that sat upon the throne said, 'Behold, I make all things new.' And He said unto me, 'Write: for these words are true and faithful.'"

That is beautiful, is it not? To us is given the description of the new heavens and earth where righteousness dwells. But -- are you convinced that you shall arrive there? Are you sure at this very moment, without any shadow of doubt, that this place is *your* place? We live in the present age; and though the end is at hand, the road before us yet looks long and treacherous. There are the snares of the wicked laid to catch our souls. Their temptations surround us along this road to glory, for the wicked would seek to lead us astray. Do you think then that you shall surely arrive at the New Jerusalem? Can you endure to the end in the face of additional threats? There is persecution along that way before one arrives in the new heavens and earth. And all the time we live on the earth, we still have a sinful flesh: a flesh which wants to enjoy this world; a flesh which falls so often into sin. Will we arrive at that glorious place described in Rev. 21?

Remember what the Psalmist said in Psalm 69? "I sink in deep mire where there is no standing: I am come into deep waters, where the floods overflow me. I am weary of my crying: my throat is dried: mine eyes fail while I wait for my God. They that hate me without a cause are more than the hairs of mine head; they that would destroy me, being mine enemies wrongfully, are mighty; then I restored that which I took not away." The Psalmist saw the terrible pitfalls along the way indeed. Psalm 38 expresses the same fact, "There is no soundness in my flesh because of thine anger; neither is there any rest in my bones because of my sin. For mine iniquities are gone over mine head: as an heavy burden they are too heavy for me." Other passages express the same idea. You get the point, do you not? Between here and heaven there is a long way which the child of God must go; a way in which there appears to be threat and danger on every hand. Will you stand fast along that entire way?

That question is the concern of this essay. We confess the truth of the perseverance of the saints. We maintain that though the way is dark and though dangers lurk on every hand, the child of God shall be preserved and shall persevere until New Jerusalem descends from the heavens.

If you have followed the series of lectures as spoken and presented now in this booklet, you would have to acknowledge that if the preceding four points of Calvinism are true, then this fifth one follows as B follows A. We confessed the truth of total depravity. We confessed the truths of unconditional election, limited atonement, irresistible grace. If those four are true, and they are, then the fifth,which is concerned with the perseverance of saints, follows. I will point that out later more definitely.

The truth of perseverance of saints is a truth so plainly scriptural that one wonders how any could question it. I hope to point out some of the most pertinent texts in this essay.

The subject we now consider is, "The Perseverance of Saints." Let us consider first, what is the perseverance of saints? In the second place, we must view its basis: how does one know that the saints shall persevere to the end? Finally, we must see the wonderful comfort of this truth.

THE TERMS USED

There are two terms in our theme: "perseverance" and "saints." We must understand them clearly. First of all, there is the term: "saints." Of whom do we speak? Sometimes one gets this wrong notion that a saint is a person far above all other normal people in the church. A saint is one who has performed a superabundance of good works and is therefore above all others to be praised. That idea comes from the Romish church, which elevates some above others, maintaining that saints, because of their superabundance of good works, can immediately enter into heaven. But this is not the Scriptural idea of a saint. According to the Word, a saint is one who is both

84

separate and separated. A saint is one chosen by the living God from all eternity through Jesus Christ our Lord. He was no better than others, but is lifted out of that miry clay of sin and death. He is regenerated, called, converted, so that now he lives in conscious union with his Lord Jesus Christ. He is separated then from this world, and is made righteous and holy. That is a saint. I do not say he is a man without sin; I do say that he is a saint for Jesus' sake. And we confess that we are numbered among those saints.

It is to those saints, though they are so imperfect on this earth, that the Word of God is addressed repeatedly. The epistles are written to the "saints" of a certain city. Of these saints we speak.

In the second place, there is the term, "perseverance." By this, we mean that one continues in the state of holiness and righteousness to which he has been elevated through the work of the Holy Spirit, and he continues in this state through all of his way through the valley of the shadow of death until he is brought finally to glory.

Perseverance suggests first of all dangers or threats to that new life which one has received. There is that which seeks to drag one down, to destroy, to take away that living faith which we confess is ours for Jesus' sake.

But perseverance likewise implies that though the dangers are present on every hand, we walk safely through them all until finally we receive exactly that glory which God has promised to us in Christ. There is one passage in Scripture which points out this truth clearly: I Corinthians 15:58. Remember it? After the apostle had spoken much of the resurrection of Christ and our resurrection in Him, Paul declares, "Therefore, my beloved brethren, be ye steadfast, unmoveable, always abounding in the work of the Lord, forasmuch as ye know that your labor is not in vain in the Lord." That is it; that is the perseverance of the saints. And though the word, "perseverance," is used only once in the Bible, the idea is found throughout Scripture including that passage in I Cor. 15.

THE ARMINIAN VIEW OF PERSEVERANCE

You are aware, I presume, that this fifth point, together with the other four points of Calvinism, was proposed overagainst the heresy known as Arminianism. There were in the years 1600 and following in the Netherlands, a group influenced by Arminius who suggested that a saint can also fall from grace. He can be a real saint; he can be holy and righteous; he can actually be regenerated — and yet fall away from grace. I will quote to you from their own works to show that this is indeed what they teach. First, I quote from the fifth article of the Remonstrance, the so-called Arminian Articles, written in 1610. Listen to it carefully. Notice how the Arminian definitely questions the truth of perseverance of saints.

> That those who are incorporated into Christ by a true faith and have thereby become partakers of his life-giving Spirit, have thereby full power to strive against Satan, sin, the world, and their own flesh, and to win the victory; it being well understood that it is ever through the assisting grace of the Holy Ghost; and that Jesus Christ assists them through his Spirit in all temptations; extends to them his hand, and if only they are ready for the conflict, and desire his help, and are not inactive, keeps them from falling, so that they, by no craft or power of Satan, can be misled nor plucked out of Christ's hands, according to the Word of Christ, John 10:28: "Neither shall any man pluck them out of my hand." But whether they are capable, through negligence, of forsaking again the first beginnings of their life in Christ, of again returning to this present evil world, of turning away from the holy doctrine which was delivered them, of losing a good conscience, of becoming devoid of grace, that must be more particularly determined out of the Holy Scripture, before we ourselves can teach it with the full persuasion of our minds.

Notice how cleverly the above is stated? The Arminian also emphasizes the assisting power of the Holy Ghost. He is careful in the article to state not that the saints DO NOT persevere, but rather that the matter is not yet clearly ascertained from Scripture.

But later the Arminian openly rejected the idea of perseverance of saints. I quote from John Wesley as given in the book, "Elements of Divinity," by Ralston, page 455.

> Can a child of God, then, go to hell? Or can a man be a child of God today, and a child of the devil tomorrow? If God is our Father once, is he not our Father always?
>
> I answer, 1. A child of God — that is, a true believer — (for he that believeth is born of God,) while he continues a true believer, cannot go to hell. 2. If a believer makes shipwreck of the faith, he is no longer a child of God; and then he may go to hell, yea, and certainly will, if he continues in unbelief. 3. If a believer may make shipwreck of the faith, then a man that believes now may be an unbeliever some time hence; yea, very possibly tomorrow; but if so, he who is a child of God today, may be a child of the devil tomorrow. For, 4. God is the Father of them that believe, so long as they believe; but the devil is the father of them that believe not, whether they did once believe or no.

The sum of all is this: If the Scriptures are true, those who are holy or righteous in the judgment of God himself; those who are endued with the faith that purifies the heart, that produces a good conscience; those who are grafted into the good olive-tree, the spiritual, invisible Church; those who are branches of the spiritual, invisible Church; those who are branches of the true vine, of whom Christ says, "I am the vine, ye are the branches;" those who so effectually know Christ as by that knowledge to have escaped the pollutions of the world; those who see the light of the glory of God in the face of Jesus Christ, and who have been made partakers of the Holy Ghost, of the witness and of the fruits of the Spirit; those who live by faith in the Son of God; those who are sanctified by the blood of the covenant, MAY NEVERTHELESS SO FALL FROM GOD AS TO PERISH EVERLASTINGLY.

Therefore let him that standeth take heed lest he fall.

The capital letters above are added. The quotation allows no doubt to remain. Words could not be plainer. A saint, says Wesley, a real living spiritual child of God can fall and finally be cast into hell though Christ died for him.

THE ARMINIAN'S PROOF-TEXTS

Of course the Arminian claims the support of Scripture. When one reads the passages which he quotes, one would begin to think that indeed the Arminian has proved his point from the Bible. I can not possibly mention all of the passages which are quoted. There are certain representative ones nevertheless which we must consider. One of them is from Hebrews 6:4-6, "For it is impossible for those who were once enlightened, and have tasted of the heavenly gift, and were made partakers of the Holy Ghost, and have tasted the good word of God, and the powers of the world to come, if they shall fall away, to renew them again unto repentance; seeing they crucify to themselves the Son of God afresh, and put him to an open shame." Does not this appear to teach a falling away of the saints? What would you say of that? These were once enlightened, tasted of the heavenly gift, they were made partakers of the Holy Ghost, etc. Does not then the Arminian correctly teach that one can fall from grace?

Another passage is Romans 11:17, 21, 22, "And if some of the branches be broken off, and thou, being a wild olive tree, were grafted in among them, and with them partaker of the root and fatness of the olive tree.... Well; because of unbelief they were broken off, and thou standest by faith. Be not highminded, but fear. For if God spared not the natural branches, take heed lest he also spare not thee. Behold therefore the goodness and severity of God: on them which fell, severity; but toward thee, goodness, if thou continue in his goodness; otherwise thou also shalt be cut off." What can one say of this passage? There is a grafting in and a cutting off. Is that not falling away of saints? The Arminian says, "Yes."

We read again in I Timothy 1:18-19, "Holding faith, and good conscience, which some having put away concerning faith have made shipwreck; of whom is Hymenaeus and Alexander; whom I have delivered unto Satan, that they may learn not to blaspheme." Some have made faith shipwreck! Now these are cast into destruction. That proves, does it not, the falling away of saints? The Arminian says, "It does."

What would you say of these texts? In the first place these passages can not mean that there is a falling away of saints. Whatever meaning they have, they can not mean that. Otherwise, some texts would conflict with and contradict hundreds of other passages of Scripture. And Scripture does not contradict itself.

One can find explanation for all these passages which are quoted. One of the simplest ways to refute all the arguments of the Arminian is to quote I John 2:19, "They went out from us but they were not of us; for if they had been of us, they would no doubt have continued with us; but they went out, that they might be made manifest that they were not all of us." That is the principal explanation for most of the passages the Arminian would use to deny perseverance of saints. Some do indeed appear to be of us; they are called "Christian"; they speak as Christians — but they depart from the church. The very fact that they left proves that they were really never of us. That is how we must understand Hebrews 6. There were those who were enlightened, etc. Were these regenerated sons of God? No; in this particular instance the text speaks of one unconverted or unregenerated. Here is one who had not fallen on his knees in sincere repentance and cried out, "Oh, God, be merciful to me a sinner." But the man of Heb. 6 is one of those who for one reason or another have affiliated with the church on earth. They have listened to the preached Word. In that sense they also tasted the good Word of God. They spoke of that Word. They were made "partakers" of the Holy Ghost. That is, these enjoyed the other means of grace given to the church: baptism and the Lord's Supper. These hypocrites pretend to be righteous and holy, until finally they reveal their true color and depart. Of these Hebrews speaks. If they fall away, it is impossible to renew them to repentance, seeing that they crucify again unto themselves the Son of God afresh and put Him to an open shame. The following verses of Hebrews 6 substantiate this idea.

Or consider the passage of Romans 11. In this text there is mentioned a cutting off from and a grafting into that olive tree. But one who reads the passage carefully, understands that the apostle is comparing what happened to the church of the old dispensation with that which takes place in the new. Throughout the old dispensation God had gathered His people from among the Jews. After Pentecost, He yet had many of His people from among the Jews, but many there were who were cut off in their generations. At the time of Pentecost whole generations of Jews were separated from the church; and the Gentiles in their generations were brought in. Now the apostle warns these Gentiles that, in their generations, faithlessness results in this: rotten branches, generations, are cut off. That happens too. Not individual saints are cut off from the living tree which is Christ, but disobedient generations which were formerly called "church," are cut off.

Or again, there is the reference to Hymenaeus and Alexander. There one notes the same thing as presented in Hebrews 6. Those men had put on a show of piety and faith. It is this pretended faith that they made shipwreck. They departed. This is not a falling away of saints, but an exposing of hypocrisy. The "Arminian" texts do not disprove the perseverance of the saints.

PERSEVERANCE AS TAUGHT IN SCRIPTURE
and the CONFESSION

May I state first of all that the Word of God throughout emphasizes that the saints must persevere. They must be stedfast, immoveable, always abounding in the work of the Lord. That is the calling of the church of Christ. It is our calling. Many passages teach this truth. In Rev. 3:11 (to the church of Philadelphia) Christ says, "Behold, I come quickly: hold that fast which thou hast, that no man take thy crown." In Phil. 2:12 we read, "Wherefore, my beloved, as ye have always obeyed, not as in my presence only, but now much more in my absence, work out your own salvation with fear and trembling."

And the Christian shall persevere. Do you want proof? Read John 5:24, "Verily, verily, I say unto you, He that heareth my word, and believeth on him that sent me, hath everlasting life, and shall not come into condemnation; but is passed from death unto life." Is that not plain? What is here true for him that heareth Christ's word and believeth? This Scripture does not state that this one might finally obtain eternal life, or that he shall conditionally receive it; but he has it already. It is his now. And that one *shall not come* into condemnation, but *is passed* from death into life. The promise is sure.

Romans 8 emphasizes the same truth. "Who shall separate us from the love of Christ?" The point that this Word of God makes is exactly this: there is nothing that can or will separate us from that love of God in Christ. Nothing.

Or read Paul's own confession in II Timothy 4:7-8, "I have fought a good fight, I have finished my course, I have kept the faith; henceforth there is laid up for me a crown of righteousness, which the Lord, the righteous judge, shall give me at that day; and not to me only, but unto all them also that love his appearing." Paul does not question whether finally the crown will be there, but he expresses the assurance that it IS laid up for him and for all the saints.

Now we should consider the confessions of the Reformed churches. In the Canons of Dordt there is an entire section treating the subject under discussion now. I will quote one pertinent article: Nine.

> Of this preservation of the elect to salvation, and of their perseverance in the faith, true believers for themselves may and do obtain assurance according to the measure of their faith, whereby they arrive at the certain persuasion, that they ever will continue true and living members of the church; and that they experience forgiveness of sins, and will at last inherit eternal life.

That is the confession of Reformed churches since 1618-1619 and even before.

PERSEVERANCE and PRESERVATION

When one speaks of the perseverance of the saints, there is one element that renders this perseverance of the saints absolutely sure, an element which may never be forgotten. One always perseveres because he is preserved by the living God — and there is no other possible reason for perseverance. If one speaks with an Arminian concerning the subject of perseverance of the saints, it is very conceivable that he would not disagree with you. The Arminian would be ready to say that there is and must be perseverance — and there will be if we remain stedfast to the end. If we continue to maintain the truth of God's Word, then we will persevere to the end. It is we who have the strength to persevere if we want to; but also we can lose that which we have and be lost. So the Arminian would also urge the saint to persevere. But he teaches then that it is really possible, and does happen, that a saint can finally be lost. We deny that such is ever possible. The saint can not fall because his preservation rests not on his own act, but on the power of the almighty God. There is much that could be emphasized to show this. One could be reminded of the fact that the attributes of God necessarily imply the sure preservation of the saint. God reveals His mercy, His love, His justice, His grace, His truth, His almighty power. Consider each of the attributes, which are all essentially one, and one must recognize that each necessarily implies that God must preserve His own people, otherwise He is not God.

CALVINISM — AN INTEGRATED WHOLE

The five points of Calvinism are closely related. One point presupposes the others. There is the subject of eternal election. According to Eph. 1:4, election is sure; it is accomplished in Christ; and it is before the foundation of the earth. If that is true, and it is, it necessarily follows that there must be preservation of the saints. God has eternally elected some; if it means anything at all, it means this: these shall surely sit before His face in glory. Deny perseverance and preservation, and election means nothing. Or reverse it: deny election, and perseverance has no meaning.

The same relationship is seen with limited or particular atonement: that Christ dies for His people and that therefore their sins are removed according to the justice and righteousness of God. Because that is true, He must preserve His people so that they do persevere to the end. If Christ's death represents power and life, so that those who are in Him are forgiven all their sins, they must also surely be taken to glory. If these for whom Christ died could nevertheless fall from grace, to that extent Christ would have died in vain. But that is impossible. With irresistible grace this is likewise true. Irresistible grace is the power of God according to which He accomplishes His good pleasure with His saints. Those who were sinners, but chosen eternally in Christ, He fashions anew. God forms them in His own image by the power of grace. Therefore, where irresistible grace is, there must also be preservation of saints. The irresistible grace of God both begins and completes our salvation.

SCRIPTURE and the CONFESSIONS EMPHASIZE PRESERVATION

Scripture contains very many passages which prove the truth that God preserves His chosen people. I will quote some of these. In Phil 1:6 the apostle states, "...He which hath begun a good work in you will perform it until the day of Jesus Christ." There are no "ifs", no "buts", no "conditions." He WILL complete it until the day of Jesus Christ. He preserves and we persevere.

Here is another passage from John 10:27-29, "My sheep hear my voice and I know them, and they follow me; and I give unto them eternal life; and they shall never perish, neither shall any man pluck them out of my hand. My Father, which gave them me, is greater than all; and no man is able to pluck them out of my Father's hand." Can there be anything clearer than that? He *gives* eternal life. What could the meaning of this be were one to adopt the Arminian concept? Does God give eternal life, and in some instances take it back again? Oh, no. Hear this: "And they SHALL NEVER perish." Do you know why? Not because these are so strong; not because they are better than anyone else. But they are in their Father's hand, and He is greater than all. No man can take the saints out of the Father's hand. No one!

In II Tim. 1:12 we read, "...for I know whom I have believed, and am persuaded that He is able to keep that which I have committed unto Him against that day." Notice how Paul speaks. He does not say, *"I* am persuaded that *I am able* to keep that which *I* have received unto that day;" but, "HE IS ABLE." That is God Who is greater than all. He keeps us in the way of life. He preserves the saints so that they are assured that they shall persevere.

Or again, read in Romans 8:29-30, "For whom He did foreknow, He also did predestinate to be conformed to the image of His Son, that He might be the firstborn among many brethren. Moreover whom He did predestinate, them He also called; and whom He called, them He also justified; and whom He justified, them He also glorified." You notice, God did not tell His church that He *maybe* will glorfy them, conditioned upon their own action; but God declares, "Your final salvation is already an accomplished fact." God foreknew; God justif*ied;* God glorif*ied.* According to the eternal counsel of God that stands. We are preserved by our God.

Many more passages could be quoted. One could point to John 17, that beautiful prayer of Christ before crucifixion, where He speaks of and prays for His own. We could read of Peter who boasted so in his own ability to stand fast though all the others forsook the Christ. Christ tells Peter, "I prayed for thee that thy faith fail not." And that was the difference between Peter and Judas Iscariot. Christ held fast to Peter and died for him. And Peter entered into glory.

Now consider again our confessions, the Canons of Dordt, articles 6 and 7.

But God, who is rich in mercy, according to his unchangeable purpose of election, does not wholly withdraw the Holy Spirit from his own people, even in their melancholy falls; nor suffers them to proceed so far as to lose the grace of adoption, and forfeit the state of justification, or to commit the sin unto death; nor does he permit them to be totally deserted, and to plunge themselves into everlasting destruction.

For in the first place, in these falls he preserves in them the incorruptible seed of regeneration from perishing, or being totally lost; and again, by his Word and Spirit, certainly and effectually renews them to repentance, to a sincere and godly sorrow for their sins, that they may seek and obtain remission in the blood of the Mediator, may again experience the favor of a reconciled God, through faith adore his mercies, and henceforward more diligently work out their own salvation with fear and trembling.

Our fathers confessed it. We must. It is the comfort, hope, assurance of the church.

THE COMFORT OF PERSEVERANCE

The idea of the perseverance of saints is not something boring, cold, and unrelated to the Christian's life. Are we possibly willing to study perseverance occasionally as a doctrine of the church, but otherwise this means nothing to us personally? God forbid. This truth is vital; it is lovely; it is comforting; it is filled with hope — nor does it lead a person into carelessness. That is one of the objections of the Arminian to this truth: he claims that this necessarily leads to carelessness in walk. If one is preserved to the end, it matters not what he does or says in his life. But if we realize that WE have to work, then we will not become careless — says the Arminian. But the Arminian is dead wrong. The truth of perseverance does not lead to carelessness. This truth of the perseverance and preservation of the saints is exactly the truth which is an incentive to the child of God to walk in all godliness and holiness before God. That is a fact. No child of God would ever say that he can sin as he pleases — for he will be preserved anyway. One who says that he may sin as he will is no Christian and gives no evidence of Christ's work in his heart. The Spirit just does not work that way. He regenerates us, giving us the life Christ merited for us; and the same Spirit leads us in a walk of godliness and holiness on the earth. We are not yet perfect. We do have the beginning of new life though, and according to that, there is the spiritual desire to serve God now while we are on the earth. Then with the apostle Paul, we truly say from the heart, "The good that I would, I do not; and the evil that I would not, that I do." Does the doctrine of perseverance lead to carelessness? To profanity? That can never be. Rather this truth must so stir us up that daily we adore only Him Who has delivered us by His own blood and keeps us by His Word and Spirit through all the way to the end when we shall surely be glorified.

This perseverance of saints is specially of comfort to us who still sin. Perseverance does not mean that we are perfect, though all our sins are blotted out through the blood of Christ. We still do sin as long as we live on the earth. But the truth we are considering in this essay does comfort us with respect to our sins. There is that way which we must travel here below. There are all kinds of dangers along that way — not the least of which is my own flesh. Daily I sin. In thought, word, and deed, I sin. Shall I assuredly then enter into heaven? Ah, I know that great though my sins are, these are purged; I shall enter into glory without doubt. Scripture is replete with examples. Remember King David — the man after God's own heart? Yet David committed some horrible sins: he committed adultery; committed murder; lied; numbered the people. These are only some of the more prominent sins of David. There was a time when David was overwhelmed because of the burden of his sins. For a time he lived in impenitence until the prophet of God came to him, pointing him to his transgressions and the way of deliverance therefrom. David knew what it was to sin against the living God; but David also knew what it was to be preserved in the faith. David, on his knees, in Ps. 51 cries out, "Cast me not away from thy Presence. Take not Thy Holy Spirit from me. Restore unto me the joy of Thy salvation and uphold me with Thy free Spirit." And God did for David — and does for all His elect. Do not forget Peter either, boastful, proud Peter, who denies Christ three times. Can you think of any sin worse? But Christ prayed for Him. Christ kept him. Peter is brought back and once more enjoys the glories of his salvation in Christ. He did not fall away from grace; he could not fall from that grace. He could sin —yes; grievously — yes; but unto death? No. Christ died for Peter. And Christ preserved him so that Peter also is now in glory.

And so one could go through the whole roster of saints. They all had their sins, sometimes grievous sins, but they are forgiven; and these saints are preserved and glorified. That is my comfort. Nothing can change this fact. Arminianism says, "I know I am a child of God today. Today I know I shall inherit eternal life. But tomorrow possibly I can not say that." But the child of God (one does not have to call him a "Calvinist") on his knees before God cries, "I know my Redeemer lives; I know that I live through Him; I know that I shall receive the crown of glory laid up in store for me. I know it." Dangers there are on every hand; threats; fears; persecutions; — but I know that I belong to Him and shall enter into that glory He has promised me.

Sometimes the question is yet asked, "Am I one of those saints who persevere to the end?" Sometimes children of God do question and wonder concerning their own final salvation. In the Christian, doubt does at times arise, sometimes to the extent that for a time we seem completely separated from all of the blessings and favors of our God. But God tells us in His Word that His people belong forever to Him. He speaks that Word and applies it to my heart by His Spirit. His Spirit with my spirit cries, "Abba, Father." When I am concerned, as I am, of my salvation; when I am concerned with the fact that I am a sinner unworthy of any blessing; I then see already the fruit of the work of the Spirit in me. The concern, real spiritual concern, for sin; the hope and longing for salvation — is the work of the Spirit. The fruit of the work of the Spirit in me is proof that I also am one of those preserved to the end. He who begins the good work in us will complete it unto the end.

Need I add: tell this to your children. Do not have anyone teach them that there is no perseverance and preservation of the saints. They will need this comfort especially today when the night is far spent and the day is at hand. Not only we, but the covenant seed must know that whatever temptations, persecutions, imprisonments, or death lie in their path, they shall also persevere to the end. They are kept in His hand; no man can take them out. Knowing all this, we can say with the apostle Paul in Romans 8:

Who shall separate us from the love of Christ? shall tribulation, or distress, or persecution, or famine, or nakedness, or peril, or sword? As it is written, For thy sake we are killed all the day long; we are accounted as sheep for the slaughter. Nay, in all these things we are more than conquerors through him that loved us.

For I am persuaded that neither death, nor life, nor angels, nor principalities, nor powers, nor things present, nor things to come, nor height, nor depth, nor any other creature shall be able to separate us from the love of God which is in Jesus Christ our Lord.